ed sheeran
a visual journey

by ED SHEERAN X PHILLIP BUTAH

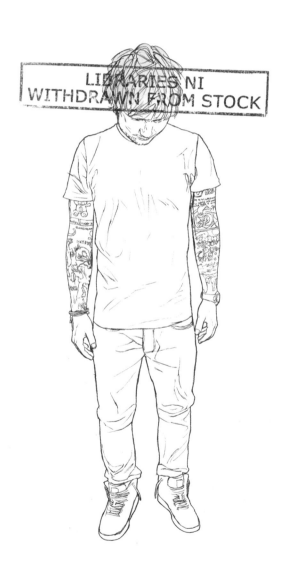

ed sheeran
a visual journey

by ED SHEERAN X PHILLIP BUTAH

 CASSELL ILLUSTRATED

An Hachette UK Company
www.hachette.co.uk

First published in Great Britain in 2014 by
Cassell, a division of Octopus Publishing Group Ltd
Endeavour House
189 Shaftesbury Avenue
London
WC2H 8JY
www.octopusbooks.co.uk

ISBN 978-1-844-03794-0

A CIP catalogue record for this book is available from the
British Library

Printed and bound in Italy

10 9 8 7 6 5 4 3 2

Commissioning editor Hannah Knowles
Designers Smith & Gilmour
Editor Pauline Bache
Copy editor Kate Moore
Senior production manager Peter Hunt

contents

foreword by Phillip Butah

Ed Sheeran: A Visual Journey was put together over six months, but the work contained in it goes back to 2007. I had to go back into some old sketchbooks to find drawings I made of Ed years ago; some I'd forgotten about. Many of the works, however, were made more recently. Doing these more up-to-date pieces has been fun. I didn't realize how much Ed had changed until I saw the different portraits sitting alongside each other. Ed is always a good subject to work with. He'll pretty much say, 'Phil, I want this or that, but ultimately do whatever you like.'

I like working that way, 'cause it's great when someone completely trusts in your abilities. When I do a sitting with Ed, he is always punctual – to the minute – he never moans or grumbles about some of the poses I ask him to hold, and he is always coming up with ideas of his own, too.

I've always believed in what the Swedish psychologist Dr K Anders Ericsson said: that you have to put 10,000 hours of deliberate practice into something to become really good at it. Ed shares that belief, too: he has put the time in, made the sacrifice – and the results are obvious. That said, he's the sort of person who would never say he's achieved the level that he wants to hit.

It's the same story with me. I've spent hours and hours working on my art, trying to get it to a level where I could be happy with it, but I still feel I have only just begun. For all Ed's incredible success, he is still young in his career and keeps improving because of his relentless work ethic. It's been so rewarding to see my work sitting alongside his music in the album and singles artwork.

I've used different styles throughout the book, to represent different times in Ed's life and career, and to reflect different emotions. Sometimes the material choice was just how I myself felt at the time; other times it was more calculated.

At the back of the book, I've written a chapter talking about how I work, which I hope will inspire any people out there who want to be artists, or who read this book and wonder whether or not to give it a go.

Ed's mum and dad really helped put this together: they went into their family albums and allowed me to use photos from their archive to work from for this book. I've known Ed's parents since I was fifteen and they have been involved in my career ever since. The great thing about Uncle John and Auntie Imogen is that whenever I call them to ask advice, to have a whine or even to ask for help, they always make themselves available, and they've never once asked for anything in return.

This might seem an unusual way to make a visual record of one of the most remarkable musicians out there today, but art has always seemed to inform Ed's journey: you just need to look back over all his early albums and mix tapes. He's grown up around it; he even has it tattooed on his body.

I'm really happy to have worked together with him to produce this unique and unusual book – and even happier to have watched it all happen first-hand. It makes me believe that dreams are achievable, no matter how big, with focused dedication and hard work. This book is a dream come true for me.

Phillip Butah, July, 2014

introduction by Ed Sheeran

Lots of people have asked me to write an autobiography, but I always say no. I'm too young – autobiographies are for people like Mick Jagger, who is seventy and has really lived. And I am not very interested in talking about my private life.

Last year, my friend, the artist Phillip Butah, mentioned the possibility of doing a book together, the idea being to produce something that brought together his artworks and the stories behind my art – my music – in an illustrated book.

We've collaborated for years, with Phil producing artwork for my albums, so it felt like a really natural thing to do.

He's drawn me since I was a kid, so some of the images in this book go way back, while others have been done over the last few months as I was recording *x* and touring.

The artworks all reflect where I've been at, musically, at a particular point in time, and they have given me the chance to look back at the way my music's developed and grown since I started out.

I've been a singer-songwriter right from the word go. I've worked hard to focus my sound and style to a point where it was just me being me, and not me striving to be anyone else. I guess that's the same with my appearance – I've never tried to be something I'm not.

It's been exciting seeing the book come together. Phillip is just an incredible human being – he's so enthusiastic about everything he does. He's very selfless, very polite; but his talent is giant. The art world can be quite false, or pretentious, but Phillip's work has emotion in it, and heart.

Every single drawing he has done of me or for my projects ties together the music and the visual perfectly; and the aim of this book is to take that idea even further.

Hope you enjoy it!

Ed Sheeran, July, 2014

above: I always remember my dad saying about Madison Square Garden: 'You haven't made it until you've played there.'

chapter one

nurturing
the spark

A creative start

I'm proof that people aren't born with talent. If you listen to my early recordings, I can't play guitar and I can't really sing or write music very well either. It's all come through practice; everything comes through practice. You start off with a little spark, and it's whether or not you nurture that spark. You have to expand it and work on it.

My parents were always interested in what I was doing. My dad's very family-oriented and my mum is a naturally loving person – they were very encouraging and I think that's key. My brother and I were taught to be creative. Our minds would not be mushed by staring at screens. Mum and Dad made sure they stimulated us, rather than leaving us to our own devices. For years we didn't have terrestrial TV in our house; we didn't even have a TV licence, because my mum didn't want us to be sat in front of the TV all the time. Instead, we'd watch one video a day – maybe *Blackadder*, *Pingu* or *The Land Before Time* – and then go off and do something else, like draw, paint… or play music.

We didn't own a video games console and I honestly think that was one of the best things my mum never did. Well, we eventually had *GoldenEye* on Nintendo 64, but only after the Playstation 2 had come out, so it was vintage by that point. *GoldenEye* was the only game that was ever in the house and it was never really played.

So all the time that my friends were playing *Grand Theft Auto*, I was sat there practising the guitar over and over and over again. To this day, I don't know what to do on an Xbox or a Playstation.

right: me at two years old.

Early influences

My mum and dad both worked in the art world. I spent a *lot* of time in art galleries as a kid. It was stimulating and I was into painting for a while, but I think I ended up being overexposed to art, which is probably why I got into music.

My parents advised and worked with contemporary artists, so our house was always top-to-bottom art on every wall. There was a lot of art in our house. That's how I got to know Phillip. My parents first met him when he was 15 and have been advising him ever since.

We would spend hours in the car going to galleries and exhibitions in Manchester and London. That's where I first listened to my dad's music collection, with my dad singing along to The Beatles, Van Morrison, Bob Dylan and Elton John. My brother and I sometimes tried to join in, but mostly we'd sit and listen to him.

The majority of my early musical influences came from my dad. He played CDs on a loop – Eric Clapton's *MTV Unplugged*, Elton John's *Madman across the Water*, Van Morrison's *Moondance* and *Irish Heartbeat*, Bob Dylan's *The Times They Are A-Changin'*, The Beatles' *Red* and *Blue* compilations, *Rubber Soul*, *Revolver*, *Sergeant Pepper* and *Let It Be*. Those albums were ingrained into my childhood.

It was my dad's brother, Bill, who got him into Dylan, Hendrix, Joni Mitchell and Van Morrison. Uncle Bill was a proper hippy back in the day. He had long hair and went to the Isle of Wight festival in 1969, which was Britain's answer to Woodstock – dancing around fires with Druids, stuff like that. Uncle Bill also taught me my very first guitar chords.

What I find really interesting is that my parents switched off from music when they met each other. They stopped listening to the radio and going to gigs. As a result, my dad's taste was purely Sixties and Seventies music when I was a kid – and there were certain people he never played, like Led Zeppelin, Pink Floyd, The Who and loads

right: some of my early musical inspirations.

of bands that other people grew up with. We never owned a Queen CD or anything by Michael Jackson. I didn't hear a Michael Jackson song until I was thirteen, and then it was 'You Rock My World'. So there were big gaps in my knowledge.

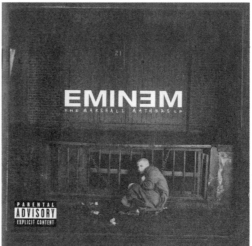

Changing tastes

Music sounds different when you're young, and you really don't know what's cool. I remember hearing 'Like A Prayer' by Madonna, which is a very well-written pop song – all the chords and melodies go in the right place, and it fits and makes you feel comfortable. Contrast that with something like 'California Love' by Tupac – listen back to it now and it's great, but those clashing chords at the beginning jar when you're a kid. I had *Hits 99* and *Now 42*. Most of the Backstreet Boys, 'N Sync and Britney Spears hits – all of those cleverly structured tunes from the Nineties – were cemented into my childhood.

When you're a kid, you don't know how songs are influencing you, but I guess they have an effect. For example, looking back, when I listened to The Beatles, I probably gravitated more towards Paul McCartney than John Lennon – towards the softer side of things and the way the chords go together in McCartney's songs. He usually wrote the ballads and I guess I was more a man for ballads.

Everything changed when I was nine and Dad bought me *The Marshall Mathers LP*. His brother Jim had told him that Eminem was the next Bob Dylan. Obviously it was not the kind of album you would normally buy for a nine-year-old but my dad said, 'He's a great lyricist. You should listen to him.'

When I heard 'Stan' for the first time, I related to it more than anything else I'd ever heard. It's an incredible song: the story, the vibe, the Dido chorus, the way it builds… just the pure anger and emotion that's in it. It's so entertaining. Most songs are stories, but this was a new and improved way of storytelling to which I'd never been exposed. It was a different concept for me, especially as I had never really listened to rap music before. When I found out that Eminem was featured on Dr Dre's album, *2001*, I bought it. Then I got into Dr Dre, then DMX and Tupac. The hip-hop influences all started there.

right: busking in Galway, Ireland, aged thirteen.

The same year I heard 'Stan', we finally got a TV licence – only to discover that there wasn't much on. It was literally *The Simpsons* and a few other shows on Friday nights. We weren't allowed to watch *The Simpsons* to begin with, because my mum thought it was like *South Park*. But when you're at school and you're going round kids' houses and watching it and asking, 'Why haven't we got that?' your parents have to relent a little bit.

I loved *The Simpsons*. I gave up singing in the church choir because I kept missing it. You can't miss *The Simpsons*. It was only on once a week, Fridays at six, followed by *The Fresh Prince of Bel Air*, *Malcolm in the Middle* and *Buffy the Vampire Slayer*. When you're nine, that line-up is much more tempting than a load of old people in church. So, I left the choir after about a year.

Laying the groundwork

After I left the church choir, I sang in the choir at school. At first I couldn't sing at all, but I improved with regular practice. I definitely think that if I hadn't done it, I wouldn't be able to sing now. No doubt. When you start doing something at a young age, it will pay off when you're older. I started playing piano young and got to grade five when I was eight, but then I stopped – and now I can't play piano to save my life. If I'd carried on playing throughout my childhood, I'm sure I'd still be able to do it.

I was force-fed classical music as a child. I think that put me off it. I know it makes me uncultured, but classical music doesn't do anything for me. It doesn't open up any inspiration for me. It doesn't excite me. It's just... nothing. That probably makes me sound like a heathen and people will look down on me for not appreciating it. But I don't get it, much in the same way that my grandparents don't get popular culture and music, and I honestly don't know if I ever will understand or appreciate it. It really turns me off.

I was eleven when I saw Eric Clapton play at the Queen's Golden Jubilee concert in June 2002. I remember him walking on stage with this rainbow-coloured Stratocaster and playing the first riff of 'Layla'. I was hooked. 'What's that song? What is it?' I'd only heard the acoustic version on the *MTV Unplugged* album. I'd never heard the original Derek and the Dominoes version, which is very different, proper rock and roll.

Two days later, I went to Cash Converters and bought a black Stratocaster copy for £30 that came with an amp. All I did for the next month was try to play that 'Layla' riff. It was the only tune I knew how to play for ages – until slowly I learned more. Now I often put the riff into one of the songs in my live set, as a nod to how it got me started.

right: Green Day's Billie Joe Armstrong, who has always been a hero of mine.

At school I got into bands like Green Day, Blink 182, The Offspring and Linkin Park – the cool bands at the time that my friends were all into. The first record I bought was *Conspiracy of One* by The Offspring. I guess I was influenced by the way their songs were put together around the same sort of chord sequence, with similar melodies riding through. But the main thing I noticed was that everyone had a band. You had an electric guitar and a band and that was you.

I thought, 'I need to find a band, because I play electric guitar.' But people weren't interested in being in a band with me. I wasn't the coolest kid. When you're eleven and you're looking up to Green Day, you're not going to jump when a really geeky ginger kid with spectacles and a massive guitar asks to be in a band with you.

It's funny that I now look quite close to how Green Day looked then – checked shirts, tattoos and messy hair. My personal style probably comes from always wanting to look like them when I was a teenager.

GREEN DAY
PLUS SPECIAL GUESTS
Thursday 18 July 2002 7.30pm
THE JUNCTION

Greenmind & The Junction present
Jack Penate + Club Goo
Red Stripe
No. 337

PAUL McCARTNEY
BACK IN THE WORLD 2003
EARLS COURT
Tuesday 22nd April 2003
BLOCK   ROW   SEAT
3   Y   52

www.junction.co.uk
James Blunt
THE JUNCTION
Fri 22 Apr 2005 7.00pm
Junction 2 The Shed
£10.00
Red Stripe

IPSWICH TOWN
MATCHDAY TICKET 2003/2004
ELTON JOHN CONCERT
Wednesday 16th June 2004
North Stand Upper Tier Area 1
Use Turnstile 28-10-41
BLOCK 1   ROW M   SEAT 0026
ADULT   PRICE   £40.00
NON SMOKING AREA
PUNCH   Nationwide   POWERGEN

PLAN B
+ Special Guests
Thursday 19th October 200
Doors 7.30pm
The Waterfront
139 - 141 King Street, Norwich
£8.50 Advance, More On The Door
PLEASE RESPECT OUR NEIGHBOURS & LEAVE THE VENUE QUIETLY THANKS.
SECURE SECURE
00300   P.T.O.   OVER 14'S ONLY

TICKET NUMBER : GA4 93
STANDING
DF CONCERTS PRESENT
JASON MRAZ
QUEENS HALL, EDINBURGH
OVER 14S/U16S WITH ADULT
DOORS 7.00PM
SUNDAY 28TH MAY 2006
ticketmaster

The Union of UEA Students
JAMIE T
PLUS SPECIAL GUESTS
Tuesday 23rd January 2007
The Waterfront
139 - 141 King Street, Norwich
Doors 7.30pm
OVER 14'S ONLY
00557
www.ueaticketbookings.co.uk

The Union of UEA Students
IMOGEN HEAP
+ SPECIAL GUESTS
Please Note: Rescheduled date and venue
Thursday 18th January 2007
The Waterfront
139 - 141 King Street, Norwich
OVER 14'S ONLY
00132
www.ueaticketbookings.co.uk

amg
ACADEMY MUSIC GROUP
CLEAR CHANNEL ENT PRESENTS
NIZLOPI
SHEPHERDS BUSH EMPIRE
SUN 22-JAN-06 DOORS 19:00
PRICE 9.50 S/C 1.60
TICKET NO GA1 244

No. 61
Joan As Police Woman
www.norwichartscentre.co.uk
Sat 17 Jun 2006 8.00pm
NAC AUDITORIUM (250) - NO SMOKING
unreserved   No. 61
Norwich Arts Centre
Box Office 01603 660352
St Benedicts Street, Norwich NR2 4PG

The Union of UEA Students
MELTDOWN LIVE
FEAT INTO FLIGHT, VANILLA KICK, MONROES, LEE GORDON
Tuesday 12th December 2006
The Waterfront
139 - 141 King Street, Norwich
OVER 14'S ONLY
00609
www.ueaticketbookings.co.uk

éistmusic.... listeners welcome
Kavanagh's, Portlaoise. Friday, January 19th 2007
Andy Irvine
Music @ 9.30
www.ovrspace.com/eistmusic
Admission: €20.00
To Ed All my best wishes Andy Irvine

Account No. 10000089
MEMBERS
ROYAL ALBERT HALL
3A Entertainment presents
ERIC CLAPTON
in concert
Tuesday, 4 May 2004
at 7:30 PM
Doors open at 6:45 PM
Door 4
Stalls H
Row 2
Seat 016
Face Value £ 55.00
Nil paid

The Union of UEA Students
CERYS MATTHEWS
+ Support
Monday 2nd October 2006
The Waterfront
139 - 141 King Street, Norwich
OVER 14'S ONLY
00216
www.ueaticketbookings.co.uk

Futuresound Present
Bell X1
THE COCKPIT
The Arches, Swinegate, Leeds
Monday 3rd April 2006
Doors 7.00pm
£7.50 Adv (s.t.b.f)
00129

Damien Rice
18th September 2004
€21 (inc. booking fee)
Doors: 2.30pm
www.damienrice.con 126
All adults must be accompanied by an
Whelans of Wexford Street

The Union of UEA Students
GUILLEMOTS
Plus Special Guests
Monday 15th May 2006
The Waterfront
139 - 141 King Street, Norwich
OVER 14'S ONLY
00415
www.ueaticketbookings.co.uk

ITB Presents
BOB DYLAN
AND HIS BAND
7.30PM FRI 21 NOV 2003
DOORS OPEN 6.00PM
BLOCK 06 C 123
£31.50
(inc. £3.00 booking fee)
VISA
NEC ARENA

Norwich Arts Centre
www.norwichartscentre.co.uk
Jack Penate
Thu 5 Apr 2007 8.00pm
NAC AUDITORIUM (250)
unreserved   No. 108
Box Office 01603 660352
St Benedicts Street, Norwich NR2 4PG

Metropolis Music presents
Ray Lamontagne
Sun, 4 Feb 2007 7:30 PM
Balcony
RR 16
CAMBRIDGE CORN EXCHANGE ARTS & ENTERTAINMENT CENTRE

The Union of UEA Students
THE HORROR
PLUS SPECIAL GUESTS
Tuesday 3rd April 2007
The Waterfront
139 - 141 King Street, Norwich
PLEASE RESPECT OUR NEIGHBOURS & LEAVE THE VENUE QUIETLY THANKS.
00599
www.ueaticketbookings.co.uk

A musical education

I wasn't the most focused child at school. It's not like I was a bad kid, but I just couldn't be bothered to turn up or do my homework. I worked very hard whenever I wanted to learn a new song, though. I would smash it out in a day and get it perfect. When I first heard Dylan's 'Don't Think Twice, It's All Right', I thought, 'I have to learn it.' The picky guitar part is very difficult to do and I spent hours and hours going over it. I wouldn't stop until I could play it.

My dad saw that I wasn't exactly stimulated by trigonometry and science and all the stuff at school, but I loved playing and watching music. It was something that I was actually passionate about and worked hard for. So, he took me to shows as often as he could, from when I was very young. I suppose that was my education – Eric Clapton at the Albert Hall, Paul McCartney at Earl's Court, and then Bob Dylan, Damien Rice, Richard Thompson, Foy Vance and, later, Nizlopi. We went to loads of gigs.

If you really listen to lyrics, you learn so much. One of my favourite lyrics ever is from 'North Country Blues', a Bob Dylan song on *The Times They Are A-Changin'* album. It's about a girl who grows up in a mining town. Her dad dies in the mine. Her brother dies in the mine. Then she marries a miner who b*****s off, leaving her with a bunch of kids and no money. Towards the end, the lyric goes, 'And the sad, silent song made the hour twice as long/ As I waited for the sun to go sinking.' It's brilliant writing.

My first gig was when I was eleven. I played 'Layla' in the school concert, accompanied by a friend on piano. I often think that if I hadn't done that, I wouldn't be where I am today. I'm not saying I was great, but I had a good reaction. It made me want to get up and do it again.

nurturing the spark

left: my bedroom door with tickets from gigs that Dad took me to.

I had a real fear of performing to begin with, though. It was a nerve thing, a barrier. I remember s***ting myself beforehand, being at home and crying to my dad, 'I don't want to do it!'

I kept thinking, 'No f***ing way am I going out in front of two hundred people and playing!' But afterwards, I thought, 'That wasn't so bad.'

My first *proper* gig was when I was twelve. It was at a youth club at the Drill Hall in my hometown, Framlingham in Suffolk. The club did 'band nights', when people from school would set up bands and play there. They've stopped the youth club now; they should start it back up again because it was actually really good. That first gig was a Battle of the Bands and I won. Killing it. I was up against a local band called the Get Together Drops. Later, they changed their name to Cheeky Cheeky, then Nosebleeds and finally The Cheek. They ended up being signed to Polydor.

After that, I still had a fear of performing, but each time I went on stage it broke down the barriers – and by my fifth gig, I was flying.

I was briefly in a band, with my friends Fred and Roly, who were brothers. We were called Rusty. We played Guns N' Roses covers for about two months – although I was really only a fan of 'Sweet Child o' Mine'. Fred sang and I played guitar, but we fell out when I got into Damien Rice. They said he was s***, I got really offended, we didn't speak for a long time and I never played with them again. But Fred's one of my best friends now.

left: my dad, who has supported me right from the start.

Turning point

From the moment I got Damien Rice's album, *O*, I was obsessed with it. I knew all the words, all the chords… Even now, I can play that album forwards and backwards. It was never off, it was always being played. Suddenly Dad noticed that I wasn't just into Guns N' Roses and Clapton.

My cousin Laura was a Damien Rice fan as well, and she lived in Dublin. In late summer 2004, she got in contact. 'He's doing an under-18s gig at a pub to 200 people!'

Not many people knew about it so we managed to get tickets. It was at Whelan's in Dublin and it started at 3pm. At the time, being a kid, Whelan's looked huge, but I've played there since and it seems a lot smaller now. It's a really intimate venue, like the Barfly in Camden or the Bedford in Balham, so it was a really special gig.

It was a turning point for me. When I saw Damien Rice standing on stage on his own with an acoustic guitar, I thought, 'OK, that looks possible. If I get an acoustic guitar, I can write songs myself. I won't need a band, I can do it all myself.'

After the concert, we met Damien Rice in the pub next door. It was a really influential meeting – not because of anything that was said, just because I met him and talked to him. I'm often asked if he said anything to inspire me. These days, when I meet a fan who is a musician, I will try to say at least one inspirational thing to them, but at the time I was not really a musician, so I didn't ask him anything interesting and he didn't spout words of wisdom at me. I just stood there, in awe of him, not saying much.

I got home from Dublin that night and started writing songs. It was the first time I'd ever written a song and I wrote six in one go. I came downstairs and said to my dad, 'Check these out!' They were terrible, but it was a start.

nurturing the spark

right: Damien Rice and me at Whelan's in Dublin.

My dad – supportive as ever – was like, 'OK, cool, this could work.' I felt so excited. I didn't think for one moment that I would go on to become a singer-songwriter like Damien Rice, I just thought, 'Oh my God, if he can do it, maybe I can do it. Now I've got an acoustic guitar, I'm just going to try.'

It wasn't a case of expressing myself artistically, because I think artistic expression comes from emotion – and the only emotion I had at that point was excitement. I'd never fallen in love or had my heart broken; I'd never had someone die in the family. It was just, 'Oh my God, pop songs!' They weren't really about anything except making words rhyme, but it was good groundwork.

And it felt great to be thirteen and cracking out these songs.

Music sounds
different
when you're
young

chapter two
finding my sound

Early recordings

To begin with, my songs were pretty random. We had a shelf of DVDs and I'd choose a film and write lyrics based on the title. One of the very first was called 'City by the Sea', after a Robert de Niro film. I've still got those songs somewhere, on the old eight-track Boss recorder that I was given for Christmas and birthday 2003–4. I guess I should plug it in sometime. The technology is pretty basic, so I might not be able to listen to them when I'm older.

Everything I did sounded like Damien Rice. He was my biggest influence for a couple of years. It wasn't just his album. I remember hearing him do a cover, with Lisa Hannigan, of 'Be My Husband' by Nina Simone, which later became a fixture in my own live set. They did it a cappella and I do a loop pedal version. It's a very bluesy song and I love singing that way.

In 2004, I made my very first album, *Spinning Man*, named after a picture that my dad had. I burnt the CDs myself and made the covers. There were fourteen songs on the album and they were all songs that rhymed. One lyric went: 'I'm a typical average teen, if you know what I mean.' There are probably twenty copies of *Spinning Man* in existence and I have nineteen of them. I don't want anyone else to get hold of a copy.

Most of the songs were about a girl called Claire. She was my first love when I was thirteen. It was a very innocent love and we only ever held hands, but it lasted a fair amount of time. Then came my first devastating break-up. Looking back, it really wasn't that bad, but at the time it was soul-shattering. When she left me, I wrote a lot of songs off the back of it – they were my first love songs.

Four of the songs on *Spinning Man* ended up on *The Orange Room* EP, which I recorded in October 2004. I called it *The Orange Room* because I wrote all the songs in my bedroom, which was orange. I saved up birthday money and other bits of cash I made

right: recording in my bedroom, which inspired the title for *The Orange Room* EP.

from doing gigs – £20 here and there – and sold an amplifier I'd bought with money from busking. That gave me the £300 I needed to send off to a professional CD-manufacturing company to have a thousand copies made. I only wanted a hundred, but it cost the same to get a thousand done.

It felt pretty cool to have a properly manufactured CD, but I probably only sold about 15 copies. I was left with boxes and boxes of unsold CDs in my room. It's ironic that I could sell them on eBay now, in minutes.

My mum's still got a stack of them, but I've banned her from selling them. Again, I don't want people to have them.

A little encouragement goes a long way

At the time, I thought my music was the best thing since sliced bread, because no one was telling me any different. My dad admits now that he was playing it to people who didn't think it was any good at all – he just never told me. He'd say, 'Yeah, keep going with it, man, yeah, come on!' That was the key, because I reckon I could easily have given up if people had discouraged me. I'm more confident now, but for years I took criticism to heart, even after I released +.

When I was fourteen I got into a band called Nizlopi, who fused the two things I loved: acoustic music and hip hop. The first song I heard was 'Fine Story', on MySpace. Next I heard 'Freedom' and then 'The JCB Song', in April 2005. After that, I became obsessed with them and went to a f***load of their concerts. I went to every single gig *and* waited around afterwards so I could meet them.

They were really inspiring. They weren't singing about s***, they were singing about stuff that actually mattered to them – and their songs were amazing. It was pure soul: the lead singer Luke Concannon bleeding his heart out on stage as he sang, just him on a guitar and John Parker on double bass as the beatbox. It was magical. They were huge stars to me.

This was all in the phase when my dad was taking me to gigs. Dad was still set in his ways and listening to his old-school music, but I'd started to introduce him to different stuff, like Oasis. The first Oasis song he ever heard was when I played him 'Wonderwall', which he thought was great. I don't think he was as taken with Justin Timberlake's *Justified*, but he was really into Nizlopi.

Towards the end of 2005, he took me to see them at the Shepherd's Bush Empire. It was a fantastic gig. The opening act was a guy called Gary Dunne, who blew me away with the way he used a loop pedal. 'This is incredible,' I thought. 'I have to get one of those.'

finding my sound

left: Phillip is really inspired by the Czech artist Alphonse Mucha, which is where the idea for this drawing of me came from.
following pages: Nizlopi at the Shepherd's Bush Empire in 2006.

Nizlopi were the ones who inspired me to craft my songwriting

I instantly saw the potential of being able to record and play back other instrument sounds while you were performing. It opened up a lot of possibilities – it meant I could do more on stage and didn't need a band. But it was tough learning how to use it and get the timing right. It took me two years to become fluid with it.

At the time, I didn't realize how far a loop pedal could take me. Actually, I still don't realize how far it can take me. It took me from pubs and clubs to Madison Square Garden – and I guess it may go even further than that.

I wrote another load of songs after the Shepherd's Bush Empire concert. I tried to emulate Nizlopi, but I don't think I got anywhere near. I just wasn't good enough to sound like them. In the process, I started to sound like me – so that was a positive thing. I took their influence and it helped me to find my sound. I also started rapping. I felt I could rap – and sing while I rapped without sounding weird – because other people were doing it.

I wrote in waves. I'd write a bunch of songs, go off and do school stuff, and then there would be another wave. The more you do, the better it gets. Writing songs and playing live is like turning on a tap in an old house: first you'll get the mud and dirty water, but the more you get it out, the quicker the good water starts flowing. I recorded a second EP, *Ed Sheeran*, in 2006. It was orange. I know – a bit of a theme going on.

Soon after I did *Ed Sheeran*, I started saving up to record the next EP, *Want Some?* My parents' art business was going badly at the time, so I couldn't borrow any money from them, but I borrowed £500 from my grandmother to go towards recording costs. She loved it – she's really cool – and I paid her back.

I remember writing a wave of about twenty songs that included 'You Need Me, I Don't Need You'. The verses I wrote then are really different to how they are now, but the chorus is still there. In the same wave, I wrote 'Let It Out', which was the first song I could play really

right: my grandmother lent me money to record this EP.

well on a loop pedal. It's not great, to be honest, but at the time it was my s***. It was the first time I thought of my own work, 'That's a well-written song.'

I also wrote a song about Nizlopi and how they inspired me, 'Two Blokes and a Double Bass'. I emailed it to them and said I was a massive fan.

When the singer replied, I went f***ing nuts. His email began with one of my lyrics: 'Sing the song, celestial man. Shake the thing your mother gave ya.' I ran downstairs yelling, 'Oh my God, Luke emailed me!'

My dream was to be their support act and hang out with them.

Want some?

Ed Sheeran

Cutting class

I was not stimulated by school whatsoever. In almost every lesson, I thought, 'This is pointless. What am I going to do with Biology, or Chemistry, or English Literature? Whatever happens I will never need any of this.'

I wasn't thinking, 'I'm going to be a world-famous rock star.' I was just thinking, 'This isn't what I want to do. I want to be writing songs and playing gigs.' Even if I wasn't successful as a performer, I was sure that I could find a job in the music industry. I could make tea at Island Records or be a studio hand, or I could end up being a songwriter, working behind the scenes.

I didn't do homework and I remember not turning up to school for a long time. I got into trouble for missing school. I had a lot of detentions and suspensions, which didn't go down well. My dad

above: playing at Talent on the Hill in Framlingham, Suffolk in 2003.

was always very supportive. My mum got cross. She thought I was throwing my life away. But from a very young age, I thought, 'All I am is a statistic for the school in the Ofsted ratings.'

So, I came out of school not really knowing that much. I'm intelligent when it comes to life lessons, but I'm definitely not intelligent on an academic level. The only subject I worked for was Music. I had an inspirational music teacher, Richard Hanley, who really encouraged me.

One day, I noticed that one of my friends had loads of band badges. I was obsessed with band badges. 'How did you get all of those?' I asked her.

'I street team,' she said.

Being a street teamer meant walking up to people at gigs and saying, 'Give me your email address and I'll give you a badge.' That was all you had to do. It was brilliant, because you'd get free tickets to gigs in return for helping to compile mailing lists.

The next day I emailed Wild UK, a promotions company, and became a street teamer for them. I did as many gigs as I could – The Horrors, Kate Nash, Natty and Jack Delauncy. I smashed it as well. I was getting seven or eight sheets of email addresses every gig. One night in 2006, Plan B came to the Norwich Waterfront with Example and Professor Green as support. Imagine those three playing the Norwich Waterfront. That was the first time I met Example.

About two months later, Luke and John from Nizlopi got in contact and said, 'We need a guitar tech. Can you come and do it?'

I thought, 'F*** this, I'm going on tour!' I was at school at the time but I still toured with them from late 2006 through 2007, setting up their equipment and changing strings at gigs around the country.

Lessons on the road

The time I spent going on tour with Nizlopi was all the education I ever needed to be a singer. Everything came from that experience: how to perform, how to handle people, how to sing and how to write songs. Damien Rice was the catalyst – he got me started – but Nizlopi were the ones who inspired me to craft my songwriting.

Luke would buy me CDs now and then. He introduced me to Tom Waits and Rory McLeod, and also bought me an Immortal Technique album, which is a very random one. Immortal Technique is an underground, political rapper from New York who writes very violent lyrics, and Luke's mad on him. Meanwhile, I was getting into grime, after buying Wiley's album *Playtime Is Over*. Grime was really exciting music – there was so much energy in the way the songs were performed and the way the words and beats were put together.

Luke and John were always very sweet to everyone. They were friendly and nice, very smiley and positive. They were having fun. It didn't seem like work to them.

One key thing was watching them perform every night. Luke is so good with crowd participation. All the things I do at my gigs now – when I split the audience in two and get people to sing this and sing that, loud and quiet – it's all learned from watching him, every single bit of it.

'Give me a support slot, please?!' I kept asking. I badgered them for ages. When they were coming to play Norwich, my hometown, they finally said, 'Yeah, you can be first on.' It was a massive deal. I was sixteen, playing Norwich Arts Centre, supporting my idols.

That was the end of school for me. So I'll never say to anyone, 'Stay in school, get your grades,' because I didn't. School is important, but A levels and university are not the be-all and end-all.

What's weird is that I dropped out of school, didn't get my A levels and didn't go to university, but I was the first one out of all my friends to own a house. The only other person out of my friends who owns a house is the same: he left school at sixteen and got a job for an insurance firm.

So many of my friends are out of work at the moment and £20,000 in debt. They've all got degrees and they can't even get a job. I have a mate who is the most amazing pianist, we played together at the first school concert I ever did. His parents wanted him to go to university and so he got a degree in European Politics. He's worked in a cafe for the last two years and doesn't know what he wants to do.

So, is getting a degree really that important? If you want to be a doctor, go off and get your degree. But you don't need one if you want to be a musician or a mechanic, work in radio or be a journalist. You might need a degree to get in the door, but to be honest if you're sixteen and you say, 'I just want to make tea,' you're already in the door. Just turn up and be the dude that makes tea. Or set up equipment and change strings, like I did.

Taking a risk

In autumn 2007, a music manager messaged me on MySpace and said, 'I really like your song, "You Break Me". Can you send me more?' 'You Break Me' was on the *Want Some?* EP. I sent him some more songs and he sent me a long email back critiquing them, essentially saying, 'No, these won't do at all.'

I remember thinking, 'You f***ing what? Like, shut up.'

Then he came back and said, 'I'll hook you up with writing sessions.'

So I went to London when I was aged sixteen and lived with a guy called Matt, whom I'd met when we did Youth Music Theatre together in Plymouth during one summer. For the next four months, I stayed either at Matt's house in Finsbury Park or the music manager's house in Fulham. When I did writing sessions in south London, I stayed in Fulham; and the rest of the time I stayed with Matt.

People think it was a really confident move to go to London at sixteen. But it was either that or stay at school, get grades, go to university and do a degree in Music, which sounds like the safe option, but isn't as safe as just taking a risk.

It wasn't a big risk, anyway. If things had gone wrong within a year of living in London, I could have just gone back to school, aged seventeen, and it wouldn't have been the worst thing in the world. I had something to fall back on.

That said, I was s*** scared when I first went to London. But it was just something I knew I had to do.

The first writing session I did was with a guy called Gordon Mills Junior. His dad was Gordon Mills, who wrote some massive Sixties hits, like 'What's New, Pussycat?' and 'It's Not Unusual'. The session was at the dad's house in Weybridge, where he used his Ivor Novello awards as doorstops.

I'd smoked from quite a young age and the first thing I noticed when I went into the studio was a stack of Marlborough Lights on the table. 'Right, we're just going to smoke and write songs,' Gordon said.

I thought, 'This is the best f***ing job in the world.' That's when I decided to go with the management company. 'If they could hook that up,' I thought, 'I'd carry on going.' Later on, I wrote 'This' with Gordon, one of the songs on *+*.

Soon, the management company were getting me writing sessions every single week, so I decided to move down to London for good. I found out about a college in east London called Access To Music. The course was only two days a week and, because my parents didn't earn over a certain amount, I would get a government grant that paid my rent for the year I was there. I thought, 'I can go there on Mondays and Tuesdays, play some songs and hang out with like-minded people – and then from Wednesday to Sunday I can do sessions in the daytime and play gigs in the evenings.'

Moving to London for good was a massive deal for me. It felt like things were finally starting to happen.

chapter three
london life

Seizing every opportunity

The day I moved down to the capital, I emailed every single London
music promoter on Musicborn.com and said, 'Hey, can I have a gig,
please?' Because when you've got nothing to do apart from two
days of college and a writing session every week, you have to make
yourself busy. I probably emailed three hundred promoters and fifty
of them got back.

On the acoustic scene, promoters always need acts on hand
just in case someone pulls out. So people would ring up and say,
'Can you come and do it last minute?'

I often did two or three gigs a night, jumping on stage at 7.30pm
at one place, at 9pm at the next and at midnight at another. I tried to
do a gig every day, because otherwise I wouldn't eat. They weren't
paid gigs – I was paid in beer, so I got very fat – but I sold my CDs
out of my rucksack. Basically, I got £400 a month from the Mills
Charity to pay my rent, and everything else was covered by CD
sales of *Ed Sheeran* and *Want Some?* I'd be making ten or twenty
pounds a day, which would pay for food, travel and whatever else.
That's how I kept going.

My first gig in London was upstairs at The Liberties, which is now
called the Camden Head. It was at a night called IKTOMS: Internet
Killed The Open-Mic Session. Kevin Molloy ran it; he's now the head
of Rockfeedback, which is kinda cool. It was so great. I loved it: I had
only done twelve or thirteen gigs in total until then, and I was so
excited that I gave a load of CDs out for free afterwards. 'Have my
CDs, everyone!'

The other acts on the bill grumbled, 'Hey, we can't afford to do
that.' I soon learned that I couldn't, either.

I shared a flat in Finsbury Park with two women; one of them was
a musician. I didn't have a TV in that flat – I didn't have much at all.
I had a bed. It was so bleak, Jesus.

right: this is one of my first promo photographs, taken at Camden Lock in 2008.

The flat was above a bar called the T-Bird which sold chips for a pound and had an open-mic night every Thursday. The World's End in Finsbury Park also had a singer-songwriter evening on Thursdays, so I could always guarantee that I would do two shows each and every Thursday: World's End, T-Bird, bed.

I did The World's End on a Sunday as well. There was another open-mic in Gypsy Hill and one in Stockwell. I did those all the time. I played at the Cobden Club in Kensal Rise several times. I was always, always playing, at any opportunity. Even if I was playing to no one, I'd make sure I was doing something. I didn't want to sit about. And it was great for getting to know people.

Every time I did a gig, I'd ask, 'Do you know any other promoters?'

Usually, they'd say, 'Cool, we can put you in touch with someone.'

Burning the candle at both ends

I didn't intend to drink a lot, but I ended up drinking every day, and drinking a lot every day. I wasn't an alcoholic, but I'd drink at gigs and I'd be drunk on stage. There was this place in Holborn called The Ivy House – it's closed down now; they're building an underground there – and I always used to play these on Tuesdays. Man, those nights were fun. The guy at the bar who ran them, used to liquor me up to get me into it. He'd bring tequila shots after every song and my half-hour set would turn into an hour-and-a-half of just getting more and more drunk and playing covers.

I remember doing a show there – a proper solo show – and just being f***ed. Afterwards, someone came up to me and said, 'That was terrible, really disappointing.'

If it had been a friend, I'd have said, 'Come on, man, it's all fun.' But it was a complete stranger. It could have been anyone. Since I really wanted to be successful, and it obviously doesn't look good if you're stumbling around on stage, I thought, 'I'm never drinking before a gig again.' And I've never drunk before a show since. Ever.

When my music course ended in the summer of 2008, I left the flat in Finsbury Park and started sofa surfing. I had it on lock. I knew where I could get a bed at a certain time of night, I knew where I could get a sofa at a certain time of night and I knew who I could call at any time to get a floor to sleep on. I didn't have anywhere to live for much of 2008 and the whole of 2009 and 2010, but somehow I made it work.

I could always call my mate Darryl and say, 'Mate, I need a place to stay,' and he'd be like, 'Cool.' I met Darryl at The Ivy House one night, when I went outside to have a cigarette. We started talking, ended up having a drink and he said, 'Do you want to come back to my place and we'll watch *Eddie Murphy Raw*?' I stayed on his sofa that night… and it went from there.

Being sociable helped. Drinking helped. Often it was just a case of getting drunk with people and saying, 'F*** it, can I stay at your house?'

That was me – drinking till late, staying on friends' sofas, playing gigs, doing sessions. I was broke but I was really happy. I was definitely living. It sometimes feels like I had the equivalent of my university years in those first two years in London. It was another turning point for me. And all those experiences had a huge influence on my songwriting.

There were some hairy periods. I spent about a week catching up on sleep on the Circle Line trains: I'd go out and play a gig, wait till five o'clock in the morning when the underground opened, sleep on the Circle Line until twelve, go to a session – and then repeat. It wasn't that bad. It's not like I was sleeping rough on the cold streets. I'd be out in a pub until late anyway. Then I'd get on the train, find a seat at the end of a row and rest my head against the divider until midday, when it was time to go off to a writing session.

Understandably, I didn't have the best personal hygiene at that point because I didn't get a chance to shower. It was just: sleep on the train, session, sweat on stage, drink, sleep on the train. I had twenty-three dreads on one side of my head from not washing my hair. My girlfriend counted them when she took them out with a comb.

I never really slept rough. There's an arch outside Buckingham Palace that has a heating duct and I spent a couple of nights there, but

london life

I was broke but
I was really happy

that was more just for fun. That's where I wrote 'Homeless' and the lines, 'It's not a homeless night for me, I'm just home less than I'd like to be.'

I lived on chips and often had to go without extras so that I could afford train tickets to my writing sessions. Travelling on the underground was expensive too. They were all good experiences though. It wasn't like, 'Oh my God, I have no money. What shall I do?' It was, 'S***, I don't have a place to stay tonight. F*** it, I'll stay here.' It was late anyway.

Following my instincts

I did about three hundred shows in the first year. I loved playing gigs, writing songs, meeting people. That's when I met Passenger, as I was just starting out on the scene. He had a very big beard and said he wouldn't shave it off until he had sold ten thousand records. I think at this point he had sold seven hundred.

Within a year of being in London, things were moving, the ball was rolling. I was setting up shows and making contacts. A lot of the singer-songwriters I gigged with inspired me. There was a guy called Jamie Woon who used the loop pedal and he definitely had an influence. I was just a sponge, soaking up stuff.

Playing live was a great testing ground for the songs. 'You Need Me, I Don't Need You', one of my earliest songs, was still evolving. I'd written the chorus at fifteen, the verses at sixteen and was always adding to it when I played it live. The weird thing about that song was that every single industry person who heard it hated it and every single fan loved it. So it was one of these confusing things, being seventeen in London and having my management say, 'You shouldn't play that, no. Don't rap, that's weird. You're not Eminem.

right: Passenger (who I met when I was starting out in London) and me playing together.

Stop using the loop pedal.' And then every time I performed it, people went f***ing nuts!

So I was like, 'Who do I listen to?' In the end, I thought, 'Well, I don't enjoy not playing it and since I'm doing it because I enjoy it, I'm just going to play it.' I learned to follow my instincts and not necessarily listen to what other people had to say. Take it in, sure, but it's not gospel.

Certain songs work really well live and 'You Need Me' is kinda my calling card. It will work wherever I am in the world, be that in a club in LA, or at a Girl-Guide gig at Wembley, playing for 10,000 girls. It has never failed, anywhere. If I'm having a tough show, I do that song and it turns things around.

Weirdly, it never really works recorded – and it almost didn't make it onto +. I still don't think it works on record. At least, it doesn't match up to the live performance.

When I wrote 'Lego House', the management suggested that I give it to Mr Hudson and make a techno tune out of it. Something similar happened with 'The City'. I always think now that if I hadn't gone through the experience of being told that 'You Need Me' and 'Lego House' weren't hits – of listening to other people's opinions and realizing they were wrong – then I wouldn't be as hard with my record label as I am now. And I'm brutal. I'll say: 'No, f*** it, this will work, do it,' rather than, 'Yes, you're right, let's do it your way.'

It is my music and it should be put out the way I want it to be. That's why it has worked: because people can tell it's not part of a marketing machine. It all comes from me.

Early collaborations

Although I ultimately left the management company I was with when I first moved to London, I have a lot to thank them for, including some great link-ups with other writers and artists.

In 2009, they organized a session for me with the producer Jake Gosling. He was working on Wiley's album and I loved Wiley. I'd worked with a few producers before I met Jake, but this felt different. He was very hip-hop orientated and everything I recorded with him sounded great. After meeting him, I stopped using other producers. I thought, 'I'm done. This is me.'

I was still up for songwriting sessions, but Jake was the only producer with whom I wanted to collaborate. First we did the *You Need Me* EP. Of the five songs on the EP, three ended up on +: 'The City', 'You Need Me, I Don't Need You' and 'Sunburn'. He let me get on with it – and I stayed at his house as well. I lived there for a bit, and ended up becoming godfather to one of his kids.

The management also hooked me up with Amy Wadge, a singer-songwriter living in Wales. I took the train to Cardiff and stayed at Amy's house, where we wrote seven songs in two days. That was great. I then saved up every spare penny from my CD sales to work with Jake on the *Songs I Wrote with Amy* EP, which was one of four EPs that I released in quick succession.

I was impatient to get a record deal. So when Island Records held a Battle of the Bands type competition in 2009, as part of their fiftieth anniversary celebrations, I went along. It was a live day in the Gibson Studios and whoever was judged to be the best artist won a contract to release a single. I played and I won. I got a single deal for 'Let It Out' and a further deal was in the picture. It looked like things were about to change. I was going to step up another level.

But it all just fizzled out. The single didn't ruffle any feathers. I wasn't that exciting, I guess. I had no buzz whatsoever going on. Island didn't come to my gigs, so they didn't see the live show, and just after they let me go, they signed Ben Howard. It was a huge anticlimax.

After the Island thing didn't work, I decided to go to university in Guildford to study Music. Then, about a week after I'd found a flat and put down a deposit for the rent, locking myself into a six-month contract, I had a phone call asking if I could go on tour with Just Jack. Lester Clayton had suggested me. Lester was a promoter and I'd been gigging with him for years.

The university said, 'Your place won't be here when you get back,' so I left. I was stuck with the flat for a while, though.

Songs I Wrote with AMY

above: an EP of some of the sessions that I did with Amy Wadge.

Getting a foot on the ladder

Touring with Just Jack was my first big leg-up. Everything about it was positive. It was a brilliant chance to promote the *You Need Me* EP and I also met my future manager, Stuart, from Rocket Music Management.

I wasn't sure about Stuart at first. I wanted to leave my current management and get a really hardcore manager who got s*** done – but Stuart seemed too nice. He's a really sound, cuddly, friendly guy. What really attracted me was that the management company was run by Elton John. I was like, 'F***ing hell, Elton John, that's wicked!'

The biggest show I played on Jack's tour was at the Shepherd's Bush Empire, where I'd seen Nizlopi play when I was fourteen. I was nervous beforehand but I felt very excited. I'd always wanted to play there. It's a good benchmark for any London act and I really enjoyed it.

The show got a lot of attention, but it didn't translate into a record deal. Stuart and I went in to see the labels and played them the songs, but all I got was rejections.

'We've already got Newton Falkner,' Sony said.

'We've already got Mumford and Sons,' said Island.

EMI weren't interested.

It was pretty disheartening.

I got some new gigs off the back of the Just Jack tour, but not many people were turning up. I was living on Stuart's couch. Nothing was really happening.

So, I started doing house gigs. I had about five hundred people on my mailing list and I emailed them all, offering to play at people's houses for £100. The deal was that they'd feed me and give me a bed for the night too.

I did one house gig in Fulham for a guy called Gareth, who said afterwards, 'When my girlfriend and I get married, you have to play at our wedding!' I promised him I would – and I've kept in touch with him. Just recently he texted me and said, 'We're getting married,' so I went and played at his house. It was really good fun.

Just before Christmas 2009, I was doing a gig at Camden Proud Galleries when my mate, who was promoting the gig, said, 'I'm doing another gig tomorrow night, if you want to come.'

I thought, 'I'll go along and play.' It was just another show.

It turned out to be the Crisis Shelter Homeless gig. It was an eye-opening experience. It was held in a warehouse where Shelter house homeless people for a week, so that no one goes cold over Christmas.

I met a woman there called Angel. I talked to her and we hung out and I played her some songs. I only met her the one time but later the guy who was running the project told me Angel's story, about her experiences of life on the street. He told me the stories of many of the people there. I was blown away by what I heard. I realized I was quite naive.

That night, I went back to the flat in Guildford and wrote 'The A Team' – the song that opened up the world to me.

right: performing at the Crisis Shelter Homeless gig, a visit to which inspired 'The A Team'.

I was blown
away by what
I heard

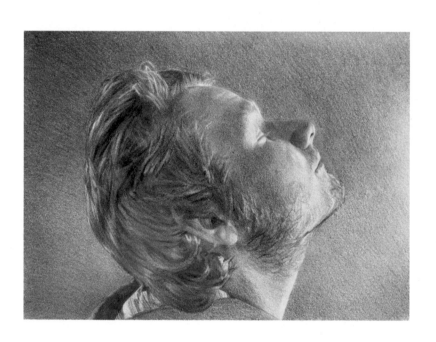

chapter four
making waves

An online audience

In early 2010, Jamal Edwards, the founder of SB.TV, tweeted, 'What's a good film to see?'

'*Precious* is good,' I tweeted.

He tweeted back, 'I've seen the video of "The City" that you did at Jake's studio.'

The video he was talking about was just a one-take shot on a camcorder that we posted just because we wanted to get it out there. I remember being so over the moon when it got to 20,000 views. Liam Tootall, who works for SB.TV, had seen it on my YouTube and sent it to Jamal. It was definitely one of the stepping stones to where I am today.

'Cool, I'd love to do one for you,' I replied.

We met at iluvlive, an urban gig night, and started hanging out from there. A few days later, I went down to Jake's with him and he filmed me playing 'The A Team' on Jake's couch, then 'You Need Me, I Don't Need You', and finally a Nizlopi cover in the train station.

There was a groundswell of interest when Jamal put up the video in February. It was the catalyst for everything that's happened since. Until that point, the record labels had said, 'Nah!'

Now it was no longer an A&R's opinion, it was a huge section of the internet going, 'This is f***ing good!'

Then the labels were saying, 'Yeah, it is,' as if they'd always known.

The ball started rolling. I was building a fan base. I'd just released the *Loose Change* EP and off the back of the SB.TV appearance I dropped a load of YouTube videos that year: 'The A Team', 'You Need Me', 'The City', 'You and I', 'Wake Me Up' and videos of me playing live at open-mic nights. I dropped so many videos in 2010 that people knew my s***. It meant I could go out and play shows and people would come.

But I still didn't have a record deal.

right: when I went on Jamal Edwards' SB.TV channel there was a huge surge of interest.

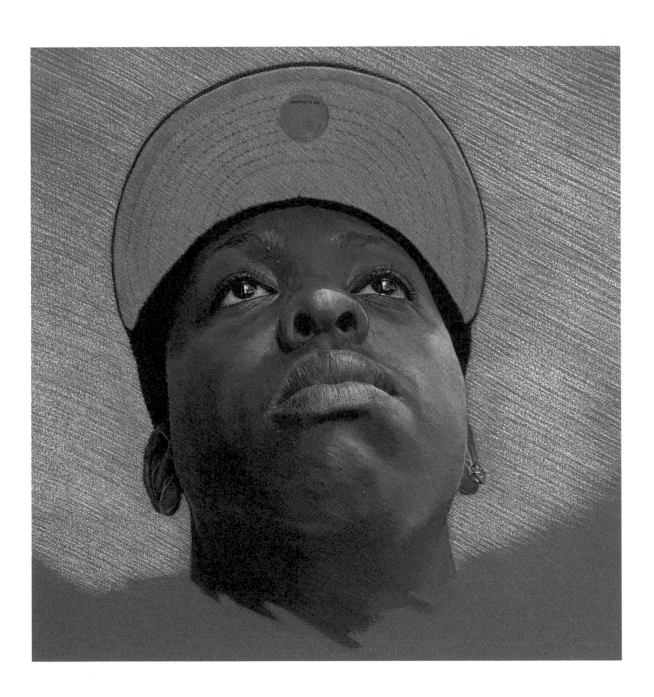

Stirring things up stateside

In April, I took the money I made from selling *Loose Change* and went to Los Angeles. I was hoping to get a writing session with James Bourne from Busted, who was living over there. Chris Leonard, the guy with whom I wrote 'Lego House', knew James and I thought, 'If I just turn up and Chris messages him, maybe I can get a session.'

First, I wanted to sort out some gigs, so that I had something of substance in case it didn't happen. A poet I knew was from LA so I asked if she had any open-mic contacts there. She put me in touch with a friend of hers called John, who ran a big poetry night called Flypoet at the Savoy Entertainment Theatre in Inglewood. He booked me in for 7 April 2010.

I landed on 6 April and went out to dinner that night with John. We went to Pinks Hot Dogs, which is a famous hot-dog place in LA. The next day, I did the gig and it was the best show I'd ever done, hands down. There's a video of it on YouTube that you can access by typing, 'Ed Sheeran Flypoet'. The reaction from the crowd was awesome and I made around $700 that night, just from selling CDs out of my rucksack at $10 a pop.

Over the next month, I played a load of urban nights. It was great because the audiences were all of a certain ilk. Regardless of money, status, race or class, they understood soul and heart and emotion. Whoever you were, whether you went on stage singing a rap song or 'The A Team', they'd connect with it. They were there to suck it up and be entertained.

I stayed in people's houses all over Inglewood and entered a community with a very family-oriented atmosphere. I played house parties, went to games nights and played poker. One dude I still see was the house photographer at the Flypoet night, who filmed the video that's on the internet. I stayed at his place for a few nights.

right: my gig at the Flypoet night was the best show I've ever done.

I kind of hopped about. At one point, I was introduced to a manager who told me he could get me a meeting at EMI. So we went for a meeting at EMI, and I stayed with him for a bit.

Fortunately for me, I was invited to play at the radio station that Jamie Foxx hosts, after his manager saw me do a gig at his club, The Foxxhole. At the radio station, Jamie said, 'Here's my email, keep in touch.' Then he emailed me later that day and said, 'Hey, do you want to come and stay?'

I thought, 'Thank Christ, yes, I would love to come and stay.'

I got in a cab and went to his house – he lives two hours out of LA, so it was $200 to get there. It was really cool though. Jamie was incredibly nice to me and I was free to do what I wanted in his recording studio. So I stayed a few nights and tracked some songs, including 'U.N.I.', which ended up on +. I never got that session with James Bourne, though! But early in 2014, I wrote a song with him for his band, so things have come full circle in the end.

Meeting Jamie Foxx wasn't the huge thing that people sometimes make it out to be, just because he's a Hollywood A-lister, but it got me interested in success again. I'd been turned down by every label in the UK, then I'd gone over to America and within a month I was attracting attention over there. Jamie offered me a deal and then Oprah was interested, really randomly. In the UK, Stuart kicked into gear, because s*** was popping off and he wanted to make sure that I was coming back to something.

I thought, 'If I can go to LA for a month and end up at a millionaire movie star's house in the hills, recording with him, imagine what I can do when I get back to the UK!'

right: Example and I got on well from the start.

Home truths

I was full of confidence and hope when I arrived back home, but – as always – things took longer than I expected.

In May, I got in touch with Example. I'd loved the rap album he'd done with Mike Skinner, so when he tweeted, 'I need a support act,' I immediately tweeted back, 'I'll do it and here's my SB.TV video.'

The grime artist JME saw it, retweeted it and said, 'Yeah, you should do it.'

Example didn't mean to take me on tour. He only gave me one support slot for the first gig, which was in Norwich. But we got on really well from the start. The first thing he said to me was something about being ginger. I said he looked like Nick Knowles and

everyone laughed at him. 'Yeah, you're all right, you are,' he said. He had a buy-on for the tour – a band that had paid to be his support act – but it didn't work out and they left, at which point he offered me their support slot.

After the tour, I got a booking agent who started booking me in for gigs. They were all-right gigs and I was getting paid for them, but people weren't necessarily turning up. I did some packed shows, but I also remember a night I did in Exeter – it was eighty pounds to get down there and I was being paid fifty pounds for the gig. Eighty pounds was a lot of money to me then, but I thought, 'I'll sell some CDs, it will be fine.'

I got there. No one turned up. The promoter said, 'We can wait another half an hour if you want.'

Still no one turned up. 'We can wait another 15 minutes if you want.' Still no one turned up.

'F*** it,' I thought, and I went on stage and played to the promoter and the sound guy.

When I got back to the train station, I'd missed the last train home. So I waited there until 5am, playing the little Gameboy I had with me, and finally got on the sleeper train back to London, where I went straight into the studio. 'Great,' I thought, 'I've just spent money to play a show to a sound man and a promoter.'

It was a knock, because I was putting everything I made from CD sales into an envelope of cash, saving up for the next EP. After *Loose Change* came *Songs I Wrote with Amy*, then *Live at the Bedford*. Whenever I did an EP with Jake, it was a grand cash, done, recorded, next one. My new project was an EP of collaborations with grime artists. It was something I'd been thinking about for a while. I remember discussing it with Phil (Butah), whose first art studio was next to Wiley's recording studio. We were always saying I should do some songs with grime artists.

A shift in direction

I'd supported a band called Mongrel, whose members included
the Arctic Monkeys' former bassist Andy, Jon and Joe from Reverend
and the Makers, Lowkey the rapper and a couple of other guys.
They did a rap collaborations album of Oasis-type music mixed
in with political hip hop. I remember listening to it and thinking,
'That's f***ing cool, but I'd like to do it with my own music.' Since
I love listening to rap music, but I also love listening to acoustic
music, I decided to fuse the two.

SB.TV is now an online platform for big pop artists as well as
breaking new talent, but early on it featured mainly grime music:
Giggs, Scorcher, Wretch, lots of underground stuff. All the grime
artists watched it. Maverick Sabre did a video for the channel
before I did, but my video was the first acoustic video on SB.TV
that got a big reaction. It changed everything for me, for Jamal
and for the UK rap scene.

Rappers weren't really working with acoustic acts then, which
I found really weird, because they do it all the time in America.
When I started to approach them about *No. 5 Collaborations Project*,
they were like, 'This is a little bit odd. I'm down to do it, but it's not
usually what I do.'

All those guys were aware of me because of SB.TV, but I had to
seek them out. 'How do I get in touch with these people?' I thought.
The answer was going to and playing at places where they would
see me – networking, I guess.

I did a gig at Camden Proud Galleries where, incidentally, they
put me on the flyer as Ed Sherrington. That night I met a promoter
called Jamie, who ran Laughing Boy with a dude called Marvin, who
also ran a comedy night called The Sunday Show. After I played
Laughing Boy, Marvin booked me for The Sunday Show. Then I
heard that Sway was going to be in the VIP area at the show. 'OK,'

I thought, 'first I'll play – and tear the house down if I can – then I'll find him and give him my number.'

The Sunday Show was one of the toughest and best crowds that I've ever played. Being an acoustic singer at a comedy night meant that I had to make an immediate impact, so I opened up with 'You Need Me', dropped some reggae vibes that I'd picked up when I was supporting the urban reggae band Laid Blak in Bristol, and then went into Damian Marley. After that I played songs like 'The A Team' and 'The City'. It went really well. The atmosphere was amazing. There was one dude who kept smashing the stage with his fist, shouting his appreciation. And I achieved my goal: I met Sway and gave him my number.

I'd met JME's sister – which led me to JME – the same night I met Jamal, when I did iluvlive. I met Devlin through touring with Example and spending loads of time with him. Devlin was very standoffish to begin with – they all were – and then he saw a show and we sort of got to know each other. I met Wiley through Jake Gosling and P-Money through Sian, who did all my press in the early days. I tweeted Dot Rotten and said, 'I want to do a song with you.' And I met Wretch at an underground station, really randomly. I was on an escalator and I yelled, 'Wretch!' and he was like, 'All right?'

Making *No. 5 Collaborations Project* was the hardest I've ever worked and the most passionate I've ever been about anything. It took two months to make. I could have done it quicker, but some of the rappers worked to their own schedules… JME, Devlin and P-Money were always on time, though.

It was so much fun, but I sweated my balls off to get it done. I'd go in for a session with Griminal at 7pm. Devlin would turn up at midnight and we'd do a session. Then, just as I was leaving at 6am, Dot Rotten would call me and say, 'What are you up to?'

'I've just finished the session.'

'Cool, well, I'm ready to do the song now.'

left: the *No. 5 Collaborations Project* artwork.

We'd go to Jake's at 8am, work on the song until 4pm and then we'd mix it and listen back to it. I was knackered, but I was driven by how exciting it was to be working with all these amazing people. I got in touch with Phil and asked him to do the *Collaborations* cover. He did a brilliant black-and-white portrait of me in biro.

The + album is cool, it does the trick and it's got some good songs on it, but from my point of view the *Collaborations* EP is the best thing that I've ever done – musically, conceptually and in terms of how it was delivered. It's not perfect, but it's really f***ing good and I'm so proud of it.

I carried the demo with me and played it to everyone I met. In September I went to see Bruno Mars at the Notting Hill Arts Club and I bumped into this girl who said, 'Hey, I'm Miranda and I'm a massive fan! Can you come and say hello to my boyfriend, Ed? He's a massive fan as well.'

I went over. 'Hey, I'm Ed, really nice to meet you.'

The gig ended and they asked me back to theirs for some food. While I was there, I played them all the songs on *Collaborations*. It turned out that Miranda was a songwriter and had written for Girls Aloud. I didn't know this Ed guy; I just thought he was really nice.

Stuart got in touch the next day. 'I heard you met Ed from Asylum,' he said.

'Oh, s***, is he an A&R?'

Ed had got excited when I played him the *Collaborations* songs and after that he came to every single London gig I did. No one else from the labels came, though. And there was no talk of a deal, from Ed or anyone.

In the meantime, I discovered there was a distribution website called TuneCore: you paid £30 and they put your songs up on iTunes worldwide. So I set up a TuneCore account, put up my EPs and left it at that – while I went on tour again, gigging wherever I was booked.

right: playing at The Waterfront in Norwich.

Hanging in there

Finally, there came a point when I wanted to quit. When I thought, 'This is horrible, this isn't going to work.'

It was December 2010 and I'd sold out Cargo in Shoreditch, the biggest show I'd ever played. There were five hundred people there. Even my dad turned up.

After the show, I was drinking with my dad and loads of other people. One by one, they started leaving. That was cool. My dad said, 'Do you mind if I get off?' and I said, 'Yeah, see you later, Dad.'

I carried on drinking, and then it was just me and the bar staff. 'We've got to go,' they said.

'Cool, safe,' I said.

I took out my phone. It was dead. I was really drunk, but very aware that I had no money on me at all. I'd spent all the cash I had buying people drinks.

'This isn't great,' I thought.

I'd worked really f***ing hard and gigged my ass off for three years. I'd released four EPs: *You Need Me*, *Loose Change*, *Songs I Wrote with Amy* and *Live at the Bedford*. I'd just played a sold-out show at Cargo, which is a big venue for an unsigned act to play. But I'd come out of it with no money, no place to live, a dead phone and nowhere to go.

In that moment, I thought, 'I've done hundreds and hundreds of shows, I've given everything that I could give to everyone, and I'm still in almost the same position as I was three years ago. Only with more rejection.'

I ended up walking to my friend Random Impulse's house in Finsbury Park. I got there at seven o'clock in the morning, went in, sat down and burst into tears.

'Dude, I can't do this anymore,' I said. I was in a proper state.

He listened. He sympathized. 'I've got something to cheer you up,' he said. 'Check this out.'

Then he brought out a scan of his unborn daughter. That was pretty cool.

In fact, there were loads of reasons to feel positive. Things were building on the internet and the booking agent was very good at promoting my shows. A few days after the Cargo gig, I did a sold-out show in front of seven hundred people at The Waterfront in Norwich. That was a great gig. So things were happening.

It's just that I was impatient for them to happen faster.

Like, now.

following pages: Phillip drew this artwork for my single 'Small Bump'.

He brought out a scan of
his unborn daughter.
That was pretty cool

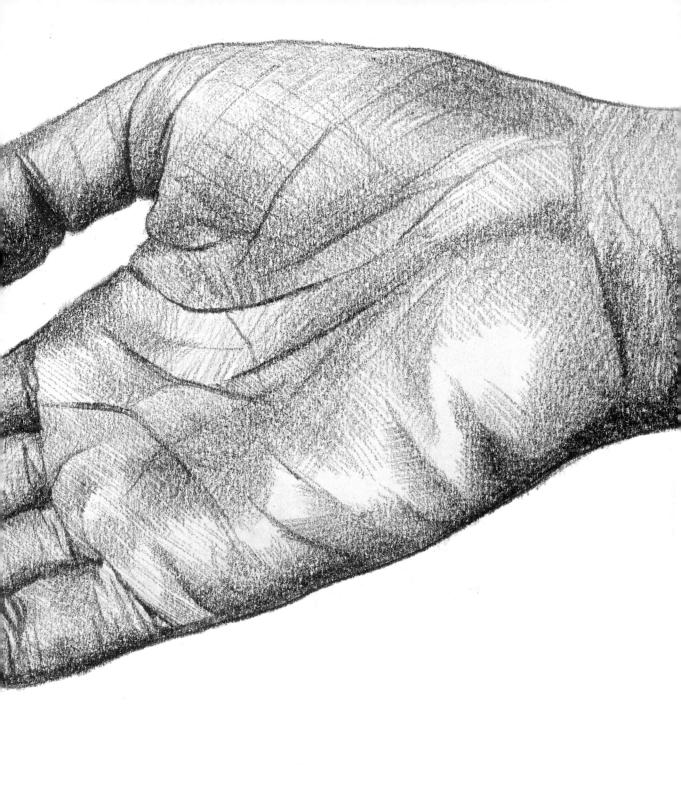

chapter five

+

Proving them wrong

I remember going into the offices of one record label with *No. 5 Collaborations Project* and asking, 'What do you think?'

'You should probably just give that out for free, to be honest,' I was told.

When someone tells you that you can't do something, take it upon yourself to prove them wrong. My other CDs were doing well on iTunes. They'd sold about ten thousand copies each and were in the chart. 'The A Team' single download was selling loads and I was doing lots of gigs. So I put *Collaborations* up on iTunes and waited to see what would happen.

I was expecting it to chart at around fifty and I would definitely have been happy with that. I would have been happier still to see it at twenty. But when it got to twelve, I started wanting it to go higher. It was at four when I went to sleep that night. In the morning, I woke up expecting it to have dropped right down, but it was at three. Then it went to two. It was a lot to take in. I felt incredibly grateful for the support of my fans.

The next day, an unknown number kept ringing me – and I don't answer unknown numbers as a rule. I'd probably had about seven missed calls before I got a text from my manager saying, 'Pick up your phone! It's Elton!' It was just mad, because I grew up listening to Elton John's music. He was ringing to say congratulations, which was cool.

Every single record label rang up that day. One label offered a blank cheque. 'You can have whatever you want,' they said. Another rang and said, 'We're ready to offer a major deal.' Most of them were offering a couple of hundred grand.

But the labels had heard these songs before. We'd gone to them with almost all the songs that ended up on the album and they had said no. Now they were saying yes. So they obviously didn't believe in the songs; they were just going along with it because everyone else believed in it.

I thought, 'If you didn't like them then, why would I go with you now?' I guess I'm just stubborn.

To be fair, I was a hard sell for the major labels. 'Here's a ginger kid who raps with a guitar.' It was not a good start. They usually follow what has been successful before – and when I was trying to get a deal, the most successful act at that time was James Blunt. I was a singer-songwriter with an acoustic guitar, but I didn't necessarily sing straight-up love songs. So they were saying, 'Sing straight-up love songs,' and I was saying, 'I can do this other stuff as well. Don't you want to hear the more original stuff?'

+

Losing to accumulate

Atlantic were the only label I didn't see before, the only label that hadn't rejected me. Atlantic have such a tough reputation. They don't sign many people. If you look at their roster, it's me, Paolo Nutini, James Blunt, Plan B, Jess Glynne and Birdy. All of their acts go the same way – bubbling... bubbling... smash! Atlantic are very particular. They only go for sure things.

Ed at Atlantic was the only industry person who kept coming to see me live. He came to every London gig and the Christmas Waterfront show in Norwich. Even though Atlantic were only offering a small amount of money – a fraction of what the other labels were offering – the team there had been interested for longer than four hours. That was the key.

As soon as Atlantic offered a deal, I went on TuneCore to take all my music down. I'd left the account to build up – I hadn't checked it, although I was aware that I'd sold ten thousand of each CD and loads of single tracks. I was expecting to see about £60,000 in my account… but there was a lot more than that. It's crazy what you can earn as an independent act.

Atlantic had offered me a £20,000 contract. I looked at the TuneCore money and I looked at the £20,000 from Atlantic. I was signing a deal that meant giving away a large percentage of my income. Was it the right thing to do?

I thought about it, and the way I saw it was that this TuneCore money had built up from me just doing my own stuff, whereas Atlantic could get me on *Later… with Jools Holland* and Radio 1; they could take me to America. If I carried on being independent, I'd be able to sell out two-hundred-capacity bars for the rest of my life and sell ten thousand CDs whenever I released, but if I signed to Atlantic, I could do a million, or four or five million.

'Lose to accumulate,' I thought.

I took the hit and accepted the £20,000. Having something in the bank already meant that I didn't have to worry about money. I didn't have to go for the blank cheque. I took all the EPs off iTunes and paid my parents' mortgage, so that was my funding gone, but then I signed a publishing deal and everything started to go well. I knew I'd be fine.

right: when I was working on and performing *+*, I had '+' on my guitar, now it's 'x'.

The making of +

Putting together + cost £10,000, which seems mental now. The costs were low because about 80 per cent of the album was already recorded. Most of the songs you hear are pretty much the original demos. Almost all I had left to do was work on the songs that I'd written but not yet recorded, which were 'Small Bump', 'Give Me Love' and 'Kiss Me'.

Up to the last minute I wasn't sure if 'You Need Me, I Don't Need You' had a place on the album. I wanted it to be there because of its history, and because the song is about staying true to yourself and following your heart: something instilled in me from an early age.

It took me a while to learn to stand my ground, though. If I'd listened to some of the advice I was given when I was starting out, I probably wouldn't have got this far. Whenever my first management told me a song wasn't good, that would be it for that song. But I went on playing 'You Need Me, I Don't Need You' – even when they advised me to stop.

So I wanted to include it. Only, it didn't sound right… until we tried it with a new drum rhythm running through it. Then it suddenly came together and I thought, 'Yes, it should go on the album.'

Most of the songs on + are love songs, written about my ex-girlfriend Alice. That's what I do, I write love songs. 'Lego House' is about that moment in a relationship when you realize where it's going and you want to save it. I tried to be creative and imaginative with the song, using Lego as a metaphor for the relationship. I was thinking about how it can take hours to build up a complex design, yet seconds to destroy it.

'U.N.I.' is also about a break-up. It focuses on the time in your life when you're about to go off to university. If you're in a relationship, you usually agree that everything will be fine, it will work out. But in my experience, it never does, and the relationship ends.

'Wake Me Up' is another song about my ex-girlfriend. I wrote it in LA, the first time I ever went there. It's about all the quirky little things you miss when a relationship is over. One of my favourite lines is, 'And I know you love *Shrek*, 'cause we've watched it twelve times.'

It's a very personal song. I remember writing it and being so proud of it. I thought it had some of the best lyrics I'd ever written.

So I take you to the beach and walk along the sand,
And I'll make you a heart pendant with a pebble held in my hand,
And I'll carve it like a necklace so the heart falls where your
   chest is,
And now a piece of me is a piece of the beach and it falls just
   where it needs to be,
And rests peacefully so you just need to breathe to feel my
   heart against yours now,
Against yours now…

But when the album came out, 'Wake Me Up' was slated in the reviews. Suddenly I thought, 'Oh, it might not be good', which is a shame.

I've gained a lot of confidence over the years, but knocks like that will stick – even now. That's why I'm so grateful for my dad's encouragement and support when I was starting to write songs. I think if back in the day someone had said, 'This isn't very good,' I would probably have stopped right then.

Looking back, 'Wake Me Up' *is* quite cheesy – but I like it because I actually did once make my ex-girlfriend a heart necklace out of a pebble I'd found on the beach. I wrote the lyric about that moment. I'm a romantic, I guess.

Obviously, some of the songs on + aren't love songs. 'The A Team' isn't a love song; and neither is 'The City', which is about not being able to get to sleep when you're in the city. And 'Small Bump' is about an

+

unborn child. The songs are based on reality and it's usually my reality, but not always. 'Kiss Me' isn't about me, funnily enough. I wrote 'Small Bump' based on an experience some close friends had. And 'The A Team' is about someone else.

Of all the songs on the album, I think I'm most proud of 'The A Team' and 'Give Me Love'. For me, it's hard to top 'Give Me Love', and 'The A Team' opened up the doors and made everything else possible for me. It won an Ivor Novello, which is definitely one of my best achievements. It doesn't get better than winning an Ivor Novello. I was up against Adele's 'Rolling in the Deep' at a point when Adele was winning everything, so I wasn't expecting it to win at all. It was a good feeling. I carried my award with me all night and stuck it on the counter of every single pub we went to.

I guess awards don't really mean anything in the grand scheme of things, though. They're just steps leading to the next thing. After twenty years of doing music, they will add up to something substantial, but on their own, they don't make or break a career. It is a building process.

As soon as we started putting the album together, I thought it would make sense to go back to Phil and ask him to draw something for the front cover. I wanted the same kind of thing that he'd done for the cover of *No. 5 Collaborations Project*. He's been drawing for me ever since. I love his work.

No one at the label thought Phil's artwork was right for the album cover, but I liked it and wanted it. No one was keen on the 'Drunk' video of me with cats either, but there have been certain things that I've been adamant about, that I've made sure have come out – and that have worked.

I'm not a 'styled' person, so it didn't make any sense to do a glossy photo shoot for the album. I make poster-boy music, but I'm not a poster boy. Meaning that I make music that girls fall in love with – but I'm not a typical teen idol with whom girls would fall in love.

I'd rather be the one behind the speakers than on the wall really.

Taking over the airwaves

When 'The A Team' went up as the first single, Radio 1 were unsure whether to play it. 'It sounds like a Radio 2 single,' they said.

'No, no, no, my fan base is really young!' I protested.

I had to convince them, so we put on a gig in Camden and I tweeted it: '7pm, Camden Barfly, free gig. First come first served, I'll try to play to as many people as possible but can't promise anything.'

Barfly can hold around two hundred people and a thousand kids turned up. It was in April, during the school holidays, and it was pandemonium outside – riot vans and s***. I did four shows that day, three inside the bar and one on the street outside.

Zane Lowe's producer came down. He was looking at the crowd and thinking, 'There are a thousand kids turning up to a tiny venue. This is everyone who listens to our show. Something's happening.'

Then Zane played the song, as did the other DJs at Radio 1, and everything kind of followed from there. It went on to be the bestselling debut single of the year in the UK, reached the top ten in loads of different countries and began creeping up the US chart after it was released stateside later in the year.

I decided to focus the videos away from myself. It was a self-conscious thing – I don't like doing photo shoots or videos because I don't like the way I look in them. I'd rather just have the music out there. I was never born to be Brad Pitt, but I feel like I was born to produce music that people get into. The other day I watched the Elton John documentary, *Tantrums and Tiaras*, and the similarities were striking. In one scene he was freaking out about doing a video and saying, 'I hate the way I look in videos. I don't like seeing myself!' I'm the same way.

I wasn't the most marketable person, but what's weird when you think about it is that there are so many big acts in the world that don't

left: performing at the Royal Albert Hall was another great career highlight.

rely on image. Look at Lionel Richie, or Jay-Z. It's interesting that Adele and I have both been such big-selling artists, yet we are never going to be marketed in the way that Beyoncé or Pixie Lott are. Record sales don't have to rely on image.

I think it was good to sell the number of records I did without it being image-based. It made the second album, *x*, so much easier. I just decided to do the same as I did the last time and make sure the music was up to scratch, without worrying too much about pristine photo shoots.

Once 'The A Team' was released, I went on tour to promote the upcoming *+* album. The first tour was in late spring 2011. I played two nights at the Borderline in London, which has a capacity of around three hundred, and similar-sized venues around the UK and Ireland. On the second night at the Borderline, Mikill Pane joined me to sing 'Little Lady' from the *No. 5 Collaborations Project*. 'Little Lady' features the chorus of 'The A Team'; it was how the song started out. That was a great night.

For the second tour in July, I played at the Scala in London and similar venues around the country, all with a capacity of around a thousand. The second single was 'You Need Me, I Don't Need You', which came out in August, followed by the album in September. The album went in at number one and sold more than a hundred thousand copies in the first week.

It was the culmination of years of writing songs and touring.

As soon as the album came out, it felt like the door had closed on the life that came before.

+

above: Mikill Pane, who joined me on the track 'Little Lady'.

Times are changing

The way that I live, the way that I am, the way that I spend my money, the things I can do… it's a totally different life now. I don't think money has changed the type of person I am. It's not so much a financial divide. But it is partly the comfort of not having to worry about buying a train ticket to Jake's tomorrow. When I went out for breakfast this morning, I didn't worry about the bill when I paid. It can't have been that much, but it's a reminder of how things have changed.

My third tour in October 2011 took me to the Shepherd's Bush Empire, the Oxford Academy, Nottingham Rock City and similar venues. Now I was playing to crowds of two thousand, which was amazing.

Playing Shepherd's Bush Empire, where my dad had taken me to see that first Nizlopi concert, reminded me of how my original goal had been to sell a hundred thousand records in the UK and play the Shepherd's Bush Empire. My goals were higher now: I wanted to sell millions of records worldwide and do an arena tour.

It was nerve-wracking every time I stepped up the venue size. I'd think, 'Can I hold an audience this big?' Then as soon as I walked off stage after the first show of the tour, I'd want to play somewhere bigger.

I really enjoy playing live. Sometimes I forget my words during a show, but I don't worry that I'm going to get stage fright. I think I'd be in the wrong job if I did. The audience give you a lot of energy. It's a definite buzz being up there in front of all those people. It depends how good the crowd is, obviously, but my crowd is usually great.

Things sped up towards the end of 2011 and I released my third single, 'Lego House', in November. Rupert Grint was in the video, which was fantastic.

+

right: playing at the Shepherd's Bush Empire make me realise how far I'd come.

As well as building my reputation as a singer, my songwriting was also attracting attention. I was already friends with One Direction when Harry asked if I had any songs that I wanted to give them. They're really cool guys. I gave them 'Moments', a song I was never going to use and was planning to give to publishers so that someone else could have it. I was there when they recorded the song and I played most of the instruments on it. I was like, 'Yeah, this is how I want it to be.' I'm quite a control freak in that way.

But… I like being in control. I'll probably get told off for saying that I see somebody like Adele as a contemporary, but I aim high now. She's not an influence musically but the *way* she built her success definitely influenced the way I did it. She used her first album as a foundation, a set-up album for her second album. In the same way, I spent three years touring *+*, going everywhere in the world. I worked non-stop to make sure that I had a solid fan base who were into it, so that when I came out with a second album, the radio stations were instantly on it – and spinning it a hundred times a day.

+

left: Harry and I were already friends when I wrote 'Moments' for One Direction.

chapter six

X

New horizons

I started writing my second album as soon as I'd finished making the first, so three years of songwriting went into it. The writing definitely came in waves – as it always does. Sometimes I'd write loads of songs… and most of the time I'd write none.

I made $+$ when I was seventeen and x at twenty-two, so the sound was obviously going to be different. It wasn't that I wanted to go in another direction – I was just writing songs in different styles and exploring different avenues. $+$ was a culmination of five years of touring and writing songs, and it opened up every door that it needed to. It just didn't push me through. I wanted my next record to push me through the doors – and I think it has. Things have gone up a level.

Eventually, I demoed seventy tunes. I chose just twelve tracks out of those seventy. I recorded them three different times with different people and then I picked the best versions. I recorded some with Rick Rubin, some with Jake Gosling, and some with Pharrell Williams.

In fact, I've been lucky enough to do lots of different sessions with some very interesting people. A key influence has been collaborating with Johnny McDaid from Snow Patrol. I met all of Snow Patrol in early 2012, when I was in Zurich doing a show for a radio station. Gary Lightbody slipped a message under my hotel room door saying he was a fan and to come for a drink. Being a massive fan of theirs, I was very keen on that idea and so I went out for drinks with them that same night.

Soon afterwards, they invited me to tour America with them. It was amazing. Snow Patrol were the perfect band with whom to tour the US for the first time. They're really good people.

On that tour, which lasted from March to May 2012, Johnny and I wrote a lot of songs together in hotel rooms. We went on writing

right: touring and writing so much has been hectic, but exciting.

together throughout 2012 and 2013, and he became one of my best friends. In my opinion, we haven't written a bad song yet.

Our writing sessions go pretty much the same way – we sit there with our instruments, come up with ideas and bat them back and forth. It's like a tennis game of ideas.

It was great to work with Johnny, because in the past I've been in writing sessions with collaborators who don't collaborate much. If they just sit there it means that I end up writing a song in the studio and giving my 'collaborator' 50 per cent for just sitting there. So now I only work with the people who I know *aren't* just going to sit there – like Johnny, Amy Wadge and Foy Vance.

I still have a great collaborative partnership with Amy Wadge. She came and stayed round my house and we wrote two songs for *x*. I also wrote some songs with Foy Vance. It doesn't make a difference to me whether I'm writing with a man or a woman. A creative brain is a creative brain.

Although *x* is a very collaborative work, there are a bunch of songs I wrote on my own: the first three, the final song and a song on the deluxe edition. I find it more exciting writing alone, but it doesn't always work. There are different formulae that you can use to make songs, but I've always found that the best songs are those that come out of nowhere.

These days, I have more choice about whom I work with, so I can also go to someone like Pharrell Williams, who clearly has a lot to give in the studio. I find that the big names like Pharrell and Rick Rubin are actually very open to ideas – because they want to try new things. They don't just want to produce the same hits over and over again.

I've also written songs for other people's projects. The Game got in contact after I tweeted about how much I liked his album, *Jesus Piece*. We went into the studio together planning to write one song, but we ended up with an album of songs. It was really fun. All kinds

left: don't tell my cat Graham I said this, but this cat would definitely beat him in a fight.

of influences came into play. I've seen *Scarface* many times and I used a line from the film in one of the songs we did: 'I've got nothing but my word and my balls, and I'm not breaking them for anybody.'

Usually, when you're working with a rapper, you do a beat and a hook, send it off, and they send it back with a rap attached to it. But The Game and I have never worked separately on a song yet. I think making a song from scratch with someone is the best way to do it. It's a lot less forced and a lot more natural.

Writing a song with Usher and Skrillex for Usher's project was a really different experience – two powerhouses in music coming up with ideas, and I was also coming up with ideas. We just bounced back and forth with ideas and got very excited. It was really fun fusing them together and making them work. Usher's an amazing singer too and the song ended up sounding really, really good.

I also wrote two songs that went on One Direction's second album; and I've written songs for films: 'I See Fire' for *The Hobbit: The Desolation of Smaug* and 'All of the Stars' for *The Fault in Our Stars*.

I wrote 'I See Fire' after I got an email from the film's director, Peter Jackson. It was four o'clock in the morning in Ibiza when it arrived and I was at a friend's wedding, so I didn't really clock it because my mind wasn't piecing things together at that point. Then I woke up in the morning, read it again and thought, 'That sounds very cool.' I wanted to be an extra in the film, just a hobbit walking around in the background, and I was happy to be involved in any way. I'm a massive fan of all the Tolkein books. So I got on a flight to New Zealand and did the song.

I wrote it from the perspective of Thorin, as he was standing on the mountain watching what was going on. I wanted to be true to the film, so I didn't try to write an out-and-out smash that would work on radio, but a song that would ease the audience out of the film and back into reality, and calm them down after the dragon goes nuts.

Breaking through

It was amazing how quickly things changed in my life. Twelve months after releasing the *No. 5 Collaborations Project* as an unsigned, independent act, I was playing venues like the Brixton Academy to crowds of up to five thousand people. I'd won Breakthrough Artist at the BT Digital Music Awards, Best Single for 'You Need Me, I Don't Need You' at the Q Awards and I'd been nominated for a Best Newcomer MOBO. In February 2012 I won two BRIT Awards for British Breakthrough and British Solo Male Artist, and in May I won the Ivor Novello. Everything was happening really quickly.

In June I performed 'The A Team' at the Queen's Diamond Jubilee concert. At the end of the show I was on stage singing with Paul

McCartney. It was incredible, to be honest. While we were doing the national anthem, Stevie Wonder was behind me – literally right behind me – playing it on his harmonica. It was such a surreal experience. And then Grace Jones told me I looked like her granddaughter, which was a compliment.

Earlier in the day, I was doing an interview with Chris Evans and there were people like Cliff Richard and Elton John milling about. Then Paul McCartney walked past. I thought, 'S***, that's Paul McCartney... wicked!'

Chris Evans said, 'You should go up and say hi to him.'

But I didn't want to be the kind of person who walks up, takes a picture, shakes his hand and walks off. I wanted to sit down and talk properly. So I carried on the conversation with Chris Evans.

Suddenly, I felt a tap on my back. I turned around and it was Paul McCartney.

'You all right?' I said.

He told me that he loved my music – and he'd first seen it on *Hollyoaks*. I think that's amazing. Paul McCartney watches *Hollyoaks*.

Later, I met the Queen, which was a real honour. There's a funny picture of me shaking her hand and she looks very happy, but in reality she didn't see my set and didn't know who I was. She said, 'Hello, how are you?' and I was like, 'What's going on? Happy Jubilee.'

Wising up, but staying young at heart

Working with Taylor Swift just kinda happened. It was quite a quick process. One day I was doing a gig in Nashville and her manager was there... and then the next minute we were writing songs

left: winning an Ivor Novello for my songwriting was a major career highlight.

together. It was daunting at first, because Taylor's obviously a great songwriter and she's won a Grammy and I haven't, but it worked out really well.

We got on from the start. We were doing a similar kind of thing on different sides of the pond and we wrote two songs quite quickly – one of them in a hotel room and the other on a trampoline. It was definitely very fun. We recorded them the next day.

Taylor likes to say that I have the wisdom of an eighty-year-old man, the conversation of a twenty-three-year-old and the sense of humour of an eight-year-old. I guess that fits. I've learned a lot about the world by touring it, I am twenty-three now, and I've got quite a childish sense of humour. She's pretty similar. I wouldn't say she had the sense of humour of an eight-year-old, but she is wise beyond her years. She's an all-rounder: a very talented songwriter, performer and entertainer, and she has a very strong drive that reflects in her global success. Unlike me, she never slips up in interviews. She always says the right thing and that's a tough thing to do. Then, when the cameras are off, she goes back to being a normal person.

I slip up in interviews all the time but I've never maintained a clean-cut image so people don't really care. I've never hidden the fact that I smoke, so if I'm pictured smoking a cigarette now, nobody says much about it. Whereas if One Direction get pictured smoking, it's world news.

The media have been pretty good to me, but a couple of odd things have happened. After three months on tour with Snow Patrol, I had to miss the last four dates to go home and see my grandad. The press rang up and asked why I was coming home early, but I didn't want to say anything. I have about thirty cousins on my granddad's side and I just thought that it wouldn't be right for them to be reading stuff about Grandad and our family in the papers, especially if it was news to them. So I kept quiet and the next day there was a story that

127

x

I'd gone into rehab. Lots of the media ran with that, so it was a bit weird. Even old school friends who knew me quite well were ringing up saying, 'Are you all right?' And yes, I was fine.

In August, I got to play 'Wish You Were Here' by Pink Floyd at the closing ceremony of the Summer Olympics 2012. That was interesting, because I didn't grow up listening to Pink Floyd and I didn't get into them until I played that show. It was definitely good for me to discover them and now I'm really into them.

I'm quite often asked if there's anyone else with whom I'd like to play live. There's nobody, really – except maybe Eric Clapton. I've really enjoyed playing with Elton John, but other than that I just take it as it comes – whoever pops up. I've played with a lot of people I didn't *intend* to play with, but the opportunities happened regardless.

Looking back, my favourite gigs are still some of the early ones, like the show at Flypoet in LA in 2010. And the best gigs I've seen are still Damien Rice when I was thirteen and Nizlopi when I was fourteen. Since then, there have been just a few really great shows – Foy Vance at Dingwall's in 2009 and Justin Timberlake at the Hollywood Palladium in LA in 2013. Bon Iver were amazing too and I'd like to see them again… but I don't think they're going to get back together.

I really enjoy travelling and that's when I listen to music – when I'm on a plane or a bus. Sometimes I listen to my own music, but only music that isn't released yet. As for other stuff, I will always have open ears, but I definitely like what I like.

right: meeting the Queen, all I could think to say was, 'What's going on? Happy Jubilee'.

On the big stage

It was totally nerve-wracking when I played my first arena,
Nottingham, on my fifth tour of the album + in autumn 2012.
I was playing to a crowd of seven thousand people – which
was really good, but before I went on stage I just didn't know
if I could hold an audience that size for two hours.

My mental preparations before a gig depend on how big the
gig is. If I've played a venue that size before, I don't really prepare,
apart from drinking quite a lot of water. And after Nottingham,
I was fine for the arena-sized audiences – it was just before the
gig that I was nervous. When I came off stage, I *only* wanted to
play arenas from then on! I went on to play the Hammersmith
Apollo and other big arenas. Now I know I won't get nervous again
until I headline a stadium, because all arenas are similar.

I did my first headline tour of America a couple of months after
my UK arena tour, playing at venues that held between six and nine
thousand people. Then came an arena tour in Australia. It was pretty
non-stop. At that point, Taylor Swift asked me to be her support on her
64-date stadium tour around the US from March to September 2013.
I was meant to be taking six months off to make the next record, so
I was faced with quite a tough choice: take a break and make the
record, or go on tour with Taylor Swift and crack America properly.

To be honest, I really wanted to get going on the new album – but
I knew I had to break the States. 'The A Team' had been nominated
for a Grammy, which was amazing, and I needed to build on that.

I had to make a very conscious decision to put in the work and I
think it was the right decision. I'm still not sure, though. I got to write
on tour and I wrote a lot of songs, but it was more stressful to do it
that way. However, it definitely made a big difference to my profile,
doing the tour with Taylor, and I'm now coming back to the US as a
very strong proposition – rather than just coming back and selling

left: at first it was intimidating performing with Taylor, but we really hit it off and her tour was lots of fun.

Things
have
gone up
a level

what most UK artists do. It helped to be nominated for another Grammy in 2014 too, this time for Best New Artist. Nonetheless, I didn't get a proper break – and it looks like I'm not going to get six months off for a while, although I'll probably get a fair bit of time to put the third record together.

I spent eighteen months straight in the US and it was a pretty influential time, I'd say. Much like England, America is a country of many cultures, so I'm not necessarily being influenced by the American way of life, but by everything I encounter over there. It's probably good that I didn't come back with an accent – and if I do use a few US slang words every now and again, I guess that's not the worst thing that can happen. I'm not sure if I will ever live there, but it's somewhere I want to continue being successful.

I enjoyed seeing America on Taylor's tour. I didn't do any sightseeing but I often went to the pool halls to play pool and drink beer. In between dates, I was living and writing at a house on a lake in Hendersonville, an hour outside of Nashville. I was really happy there, so I didn't delve into Nashville much. Johnny McDaid came out and we built a studio in the basement, which was cool. Whenever friends came round, they'd jump in the lake, but I have a perforated eardrum and can't put my head underwater unless I put in earplugs and wear a hat, which was something I didn't really want to do. Later in the year, Johnny and I got a house in LA. We did a bunch of songs, five for the new album.

Working with Pharrell happened because I was a fan of the work he had done for other artists and I wanted to see if we could do something together. I didn't know what would come out of it.

When it came to the session, I was apprehensive to begin with. I didn't really like anything that he was coming up with. He played me one thing that he was very keen on doing and I said, 'No.'

Then I started playing the riff on the guitar and he said, 'Give it a try.' I gave it a try and the song just came together bit by bit.

right: Phillip did this drawing to mark my collaboration with Pharrell on 'Sing'.
following pages: practising just before a show at the Royal Albert Hall in March 2014.

It sounded great by the end. That was pretty much the whole session and the result was 'Sing'.

In songwriting, after the melody comes the rhythm to the melody, and the words will kind of present themselves to fit the rhythm. I don't really analyse how it happens. Sometimes it works; sometimes it doesn't. I wrote the lyrics to 'Sing' there and then, in the session, and they were based on a scene from real life.

I've never written anything that hasn't been about a real scene, other than the song for *The Hobbit: The Desolation of Smaug*.

Enjoying the ride

So this really is an exciting time for me. I'm getting to do some very fun things.

I played with Elton John at the Grammys 2013 and at Elton's AIDS Foundation 2014 Oscars party as well. I played 'The A Team' at the former and 'Candle in the Wind' at the latter. I really wanted to play at the Grammys and they said I couldn't unless I played a duet with someone. Then Elton suggested we do it together. It was amazing, a phenomenal experience.

I went to about four Oscars parties, including two after-event parties. Things like that are quite fun to do but they don't add to the music. They're just payoffs, perks of the job, but none of them influence me musically. I guess I might have an experience that influences a song, but that's incidental. I don't write songs about my public persona. No one can relate to songs about how hard it is to be famous. I think it's best to stick to things that you can relate to yourself as a person, not as a celebrity – to write songs about love, hatred, pain, death and all that sort of stuff.

right: Elton's been a great support; this is us playing together at the Grammys.

I don't worry about losing touch with ordinary life because when I'm not on tour I live in the middle of the countryside, where all my friends are. So one day I'll be at a film star's home in Malibu and the next day I'll be at the local pub in Suffolk. And when I get home I turn back into the person I was before and no one treats me differently.

In five years' time I'd love to be writing for other people, adding something to their music. I'd like to be constantly playing with people I admire and I'd like to have a loyal fan base that comes to my shows. It's interesting that artists like Elton John and Paul McCartney are still touring and still hungry to create new music and be successful. I'm not sure if I will have the same hunger in twenty years' time. I probably will, but I'm not planning that far ahead.

What I'd really like to do is settle down and have a family, maybe after the fourth or fifth album. But right now I'm concentrating on the immediate future – and my main ambition is to play a stadium and to sell more copies of *x* than I did of *+*.

Then to do the same with the next record. Hopefully.

X

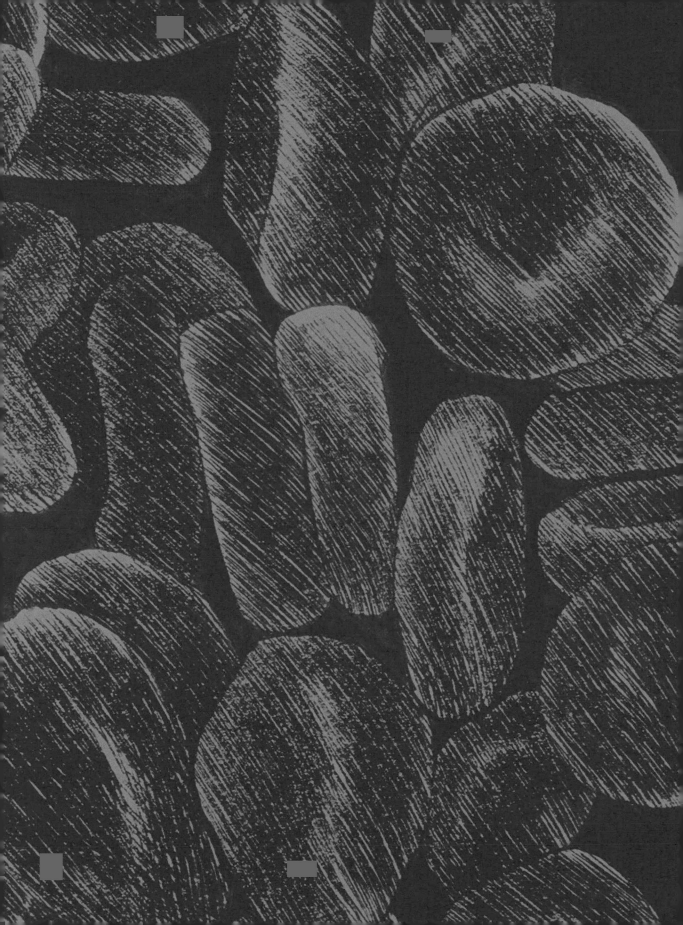

chapter seven

keeping the
flame burning

Nothing ventured, nothing gained

My dad always said, 'Nothing ventured, nothing gained,' and I still walk into every situation with that motto in mind. It's a 'What have I got to lose?' attitude, even with big things people don't think are remotely possible. That's why I booked three Madison Square Garden dates in 2013. The worst thing that could have happened was that I wouldn't sell out the first date, while the best thing was that I would sell out all three nights and have the whole US music industry talking about it and wondering how the f*** I had managed it. So I take that approach with everything I do musically.

I always remember my dad going on about this Madison Square Garden place in New York, basically telling me about all the amazing concerts and boxing matches that went on there. When I first started playing music, he said, 'You haven't made it until you've played there.'

The call of America

I honestly never thought I would even release an album in America, let alone break it. I remember sitting on the steps of the 9:30 Club in Washington with my agent, just after I'd opened up for Snow Patrol that night, and asking him if Madison Square Garden was ever going to be a possibility. He said that we would look at booking it when we got to album two or three, and it was definitely something to work towards…

left: I guess at the end of the day it's just about me, my guitar, the music and the audience.

Then came the day we sold out all three Madison Square Garden dates and he emailed me to let me know – and I was still on album one. It was a crazy feeling, but so amazing. It was especially brilliant to have so many friends and family come to the gigs and celebrate everything we had achieved. They had all played such a massive part in my career.

People think it's really hard to break America. It is and it isn't. You just have to put in the work. It's easy to have one hit there – you go there, do the radio rounds, do the TV interviews, the song blows up and then you come back to England and say, 'I had a hit in America!' But to sustain it, you have to stay there. You need to have a constant presence. It's like playing keepy-uppy with a football – the moment you take your foot away, it's gone. You just have to keep going there and reminding people, bringing out new music and keeping up the hype. That's the hard bit, I guess.

Australia is another big market and it's my favourite place to visit, because everyone's got a sense of humour there – they're all mad.

Learning from the best

I don't always listen to advice, but there are certain people whose opinion I value. It was thanks to them that 'Sing' was released when it was.

'Sing' wasn't even going to be on *x* originally – I was saving it for another album that I was going to do mostly with Pharrell Williams, something with a funkier sound. Pharrell is such a great person to work with. Even the way he talks is soulful; you feel like you're learning infinite wisdom when you have a conversation with him. He's really nice and very humble. I find myself playing compliment tennis with him. He'll never take a compliment; he'll just bash one right back at you. So I was planning on a major collaboration with him before 'Sing' was released. But whenever anyone heard it, they said, 'That should be on x. You should release it as a single.'

Elton John first planted the seed when he came in to the office to listen to the album and I also played him 'Sing'. 'You're mental if you don't put that on the album' were his words.

About a month later, I went out to dinner with Pharrell and he suggested that 'Sing' would make a great first single. And then Taylor Swift said I'd be mad to put out 'One' first, as I'd originally planned. She said, 'That's just gonna… not bore people, but just satisfy them.'

Taylor and Elton are two of the people whose opinions I really listen to when it comes to my music. I played Taylor every song I wrote for my second album. She has never put a foot wrong in the advice she's given me. And she was right about 'Sing'. Everyone's got an opinion about it – they either hate it or love it, but at least they're talking about it. It's the furthest left I went on the second album and it shocked people. If I'd released 'One' as the first single, it wouldn't have had the same impact – and I just thought the lead single should have a bit more punch. It was my first UK number one, which was great.

Writing *x*

'Sing' is probably not representative of the whole album. There are a lot of songs in that vein, although I think they lean more towards R&B than disco, but *x* is a mixture of a lot of things. It's definitely a step forward for me musically.

The first album was melancholic and relaxed and there's still a lot of that on the second album, but it's also got something different. I started off making an acoustic record … and it turned into a neo-soul funk record! I'd say that the ideal environment to listen to it is in your bedroom, on the train, walking – just somewhere on your own.

While I was writing the second album, I was travelling and taking in a lot of influences. I was pulled in many different directions. I was given a lot of opportunities to work with musicians and producers who took me out of my comfort zone and encouraged me to try something new; I spent a lot of time with hip-hop producers and ended up experimenting.

Please yourself, the rest will follow

One thing I didn't do was to set out to please anyone – when you start trying to please your fanbase, that's probably when things go downhill. Bill Cosby said, 'The key to failure is to try and please everyone.' Why bother to please everyone? Please yourself. The rest will follow. I'm always going to write what I want, even if people don't like it.

This time around I didn't care all that much about getting bad reviews in the press. When *+* came out, I was younger and less experienced, and getting criticized didn't go down too well.

I think I got about two good reviews in the mainstream press. The rest were mixed and some were plain bad. After I had come out the other side and sold five million albums, it didn't matter so much. If you can sell five million albums off the back of bad reviews, you can't really complain.

There was a lot of speculation about the second single from *x*, 'Don't'. Basically, I said what I wanted to say when I wrote it and now I think the less I speak about it the better. The song is there and people can make up their own minds about it.

My favourite song on *x* is the last song that went on it, track eleven: 'Thinking Out Loud'. I wrote it in my kitchen and recorded it that week – the album was complete, but then we added it. I like it because it's actually the only happy song on the album.

People think I must be a sad guy because I write lots of sad songs, but you have to remember that when you're happy, you're not going to be in a dark hotel room writing a song. You're going to be out having fun. The only times you do write songs are when you're in dark hotel rooms – and that's why they can be a bit melancholy.

I'm still learning

My dad always said, 'If you don't actually need to do a degree to get a job, then go out and experience it.' If you're going to be a musician, your education is going to come from writing songs, doing shows, practising, meeting people and networking. My advice would be to start doing that as early as possible. When I was at school, I was often writing a song or two a day – sometimes five songs a day – just getting these songs out of me.

Fans ask me all the time for some words of wisdom, but I'm not sure I'm really the best person to ask for advice. I enjoyed doing a guest stint on *The Voice USA* as a mentor, but I also felt that I had only really been in this big successful music world for three years – and although I've been doing music for twelve years in total, I didn't have a lot in the form of solid advice to offer these kids. (I say kids, but half of them were older than me.) I didn't want to come across as a know-it-all, because I'm still learning myself, so I just spoke about anything I'd done that I thought might be useful to them.

When I'm asked for my advice on how to break into the music industry, I always say, write as many songs as possible and play as many shows as you can. The first songs and shows you write and do will always be terrible, but you have to get those bad ones out of the way and refine your talent to a point where you start writing and playing good stuff every day. Now and then there will be a bad song or a bad show, but just get it finished, and move on – otherwise your next song or next show will have a bit of the bad one left in it. So always finish your bad songs, and learn from your bad shows.

Keep your eyes and ears open

It's an old saying, 'Practice makes perfect,' but there's truth in it. The more you write songs, the better they will be. Listen to other people's songs too and don't be afraid to take influence from everywhere, because everyone does it. You need to play shows anywhere and everywhere, to learn how to work a crowd. But never try to please people for the sake of it. You should do your own thing and do it because you enjoy it.

I think it's quite healthy to be a little bit cautious when you come into the music industry. I came into it wide-eyed, thinking that everything was great and everyone was my friend. The more you get into it, the more you realize it's not quite like that. You need to stay alert to that.

Just be you. That's the best advice I can give. There are seven billion people in this world and there is no one like you. There is no one who is going to write songs like you and there's no one who is going to sound like you, as long as you tap into yourself. You can imitate people to a point, if it helps you to write songs, play guitar and sing, but once you've found your voice, stick with it, even if people are telling you it sounds odd and won't work. Just keep on doing it, and eventually it will work.

I know that the music I make comes from my heart and soul – and if that makes me a 'sensitive' singer-songwriter, then so be it. I'm just making the music I want to make and working as hard as I can to try and put it out.

My image probably isn't going to improve with age – but my songs will, so that's a good thing.

Working with others

Collaboration is key. We can't all know everything, but we can
be masters of our own craft – and if you fuse with someone who
is a master of theirs, you can create some really cool stuff that you
wouldn't have created otherwise. So collaborate as much as you
can with people you want to work with, but don't dilute yourself
for the sake of it. Learn when to say no.

Collaborating with producers and artists has been crucial for
me. Working with Rick Rubin, for instance, made all the difference
to *x*. I'd been working on the album for two years and I was kind
of done; I couldn't be bothered with it any more. Yet it re-energized
me to work with someone like him. He revamped everything.
We recorded the songs in more interesting ways, did it all live
and made it more raw.

Working with Pharrell was a very interesting experience too.
He works in all these different chord modes and he loves jazz,
whereas jazz is something I've never really got my head around.
I'm definitely more into melodies and sounds that have a certain
calmness about them; jazz can be quite on edge at times. It was
great to have that input and influence from him. He's a genius.

Writing other people's hits is lovely – but it can be quite
frustrating because I'll think, 'If I'd have known that would be
a hit, I'd have kept it for myself!'

Still, building a reputation as a songwriter as well as an artist
is very important to me, so I'm usually pretty happy when one
of my songs is a hit, even if I'm not singing it.

Future ambitions

I would love to write more songs for films in the future. Johnny McDaid and I wrote the end credit song 'All Of The Stars' for the movie *The Fault in Our Stars*, and that was great to do. The movie and the book are quite emotive, and I guess people think of me as writing emotive songs, so that's probably why I was asked to do it. I have always wanted to do a whole film soundtrack like Badly Drawn Boy has done, but it's all about finding the right film.

I have an ambition to start my own label one day and I'm sure it will happen, sometime in the future. I just need to find the right artists; people to whom I want to devote a lot of time and effort. But for now I'm devoting all my time to making my own stuff work first.

Living the dream

Nothing about fame has surprised me. It's everything people said it would be, good and bad. Luckily, no one gives a s*** about my personal life, so I don't get the kind of attention that other people have to put up with. That life is completely different to mine – being followed around by the paparazzi and having that adoration and spotlight thing. I've never had it yet. I might have it one day and be able to relate to it, but at the moment it's not really me.

I lived out a very cool dream when I was asked to perform a song at The Beatles' 50th anniversary TV special in America in February 2014. I chose 'In My Life' because I wanted to play a quiet acoustic song in the midst of so many big band numbers, but I also thought someone else would choose 'Yesterday' and probably sing it better than me.

It was an incredible experience, just to be playing on the same stage as people that meant so much – not just to me, but also to my mum and dad. It's so strange to think I grew up listening to them and so did my parents. It was a surreal experience all round, but definitely one I will remember. How amazing that I'll be able to tell my grandkids I had a margarita with McCartney and got him to sign a rare 1960s Höfner bass guitar for me. He wrote: 'For Ed who is brilliant!'

Always looking ahead

X going to number 1 in the UK and USA on release was unbelievable, but it didn't make me any less driven. I started my third album the day I handed in my second, just like I did with the second when I finished the first. I always want to have something I'm working towards. It's tough to sit down and write songs when you're on a promo run, just because it's so intense, but I'm definitely storing a lot of ideas.

I'm now just trying to work out which album in my series to do next, but once I've decided, it'll be full steam ahead. One thing I was told, back when I was just starting to make it, was that when you become successful, you live out every dream you have for yourself in a matter of months – so you constantly have to make new dreams. I've definitely found that to be true.

I keep having to make new dreams and I'm enjoying every second of it. It's very cool to be in a job where you make people happy every day.

keeping the flame burning

above: soundchecking just before performing at the Royal Albert Hall.

discography of UK releases

January 2005 – *The Orange Room* EP
March 2006 – *Ed Sheeran* EP
June 2007 – *Want Some?* EP
November 2009 – *You Need Me* EP
February 2010 – *Loose Change* EP
June 2010 – *Songs I Wrote with Amy* EP
December 2010 – *Live at the Bedford* EP
January 2011 – *No. 5 Collaborations
  Project* EP
April 2011 – *One Take* EP
June 2011 – 'The A Team' single
August 2011 – 'You Need Me, I Don't
  Need You' single
September 2011 – + album
November 2011 – 'Lego House' single
December 2011 – *Thank You* EP
February 2012 – *The Slumdon Bridge* EP
February 2012 – 'Drunk' single
May 2012 – 'Small Bump' single
November 2012 – 'Give Me Love' single
November 2013 – 'I See Fire' released on
  The Hobbit: The Desolation of Smaug OST
April 2014 – 'Sing' single
June 2014 – x album

It's very cool
    to be in a job where you
make people happy every day

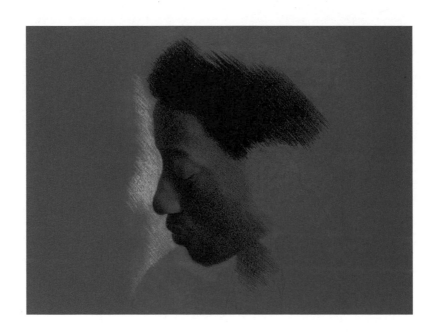

how the artist works
by Phillip Butah

Working with Ed

Ed's probably forgotten this, but just around the time he started gigging in London, he came round to my house and we started talking about how we'd like to work on something together.

'What could we do?' I asked.

By then, I'd been drawing him for a while. I liked drawing Ed because he was always up for it. Having grown up around art, he understood it. I never had to say, 'Can I draw you?' It just happened naturally – he'd be playing his guitar and singing, and I'd be drawing.

'We should do a book,' he said, that afternoon.
'Yeah!' I said.

Then we forgot about it.

A couple of years later, I called my sister and said, 'Remember that book I wanted to do with Ed? I think I should do it.'
I still didn't know how it should be done or what it would be about. I just knew I wanted to do it.

Mutual support

Ed represents a lot, not just to me personally, but culturally. I can't think of anyone else who can go from a club in LA to Buckingham Palace and be loved equally in both worlds. When he's playing on stage, there's a real purity about it – and that's why I think people love him so much, because it's real. He seems to have absorbed all the music he's

page 164: *Self portrait.* It's kind of awkward drawing yourself looking down! I did it with the help of a very tall mirror, which is how I captured this angle.

ever heard, from when he was a small child. Now he can mix with so many different musical genres – grime, hip hop, folk and rock.

On a personal level, he's just a good guy, a genuine person. I see him as a younger brother, so his success feels like my success. I'm so proud of him. I respect him so much. He has worked incredibly hard to get to where he is and he's always remained so humble throughout. I know, because I was there when he was gigging in the early days. I was there when he was recording demos in the studio and he said, 'Phil, is it really going to work for me?'

'Bro, you're going to be huge,' I said, with absolute confidence.

In the same way, when I was having doubts about what I was doing, Ed was like, 'Phil, you're amazing. I've grown up around so much art, and you are one of the best I've seen. So trust me when I say that. Just keep at it.' This was a much younger guy telling me not to give up, but it really helped. It was just a quick thing, but sometimes that's all you need. You don't need the whole therapy session.

Artistic collaboration

I can't remember the first time I met Ed, but it must have been around the time I met his parents, John and Imogen, in 1998, while I was still at secondary school. They were putting together the exhibition and catalogue for a national art competition I had entered – The Prince of Wales's Young Artists' Award. They've been instrumental in my career ever since.

I haven't been drawing Ed consistently in all that time. There have been huge gaps over the years, partly because I didn't always take my sketchbook with me when I went to see him. Other times I was

following pages: *Asher D* (Ashley Walters). After I saw the film *Bullet Boy*, I thought, 'I've got to draw this guy.' He liked what I did so much that he asked me to do a portrait for his rap album. He's the nicest guy, and he has an amazing face.

too busy tapping my feet to concentrate. I guess it really picked up when he asked me to draw the cover of the *No. 5 Collaborations Project*. I was nervous about doing it at first, but Ed was so cool and laid-back about it. 'This is going to be great,' he said, encouragingly.

I was so excited to be part of it. It was such a chilled environment that I didn't feel any pressure at all. Ed knows that I'm going to do what I do and he leaves me to it. I love working that way.

This book has taken about six months to create. It's been difficult to get done, because Ed is global now, he is huge, so I've only had time to draw him as and when. He just doesn't have very much time to himself anymore. It's rush, rush, rush for him.

When I do see him, I just have to get it together and draw. Sometimes I'm a bit slow at the beginning, but I always get into it. One time I was working so fast that by the end of the session I'd pretty much finished the portrait. 'It's done now!'

Early days

I was always drawing, even as a little kid. My earliest memories all involve me drawing. When I was four, my teacher in Reception said to my mum: 'You've got a gifted child.'

Early on, I had an eye for detail. The other kids would ask me to draw their stickmen for them and instead of drawing a curly scribble for hair, I'd notice the actual hair length and reproduce it. My noses had nostrils, my eyes had eyebrows and eyelashes – I was doing all that stuff from the start. I was always into drawing people's faces.

Towards the end of my time at primary school, I started a little business making illustrated bookmarks and selling them to the other kids. Then the teachers started asking me to draw their pets

– they paid me in art materials, which was great and encouraging. They were very supportive, as were my family, and it wasn't long before I got into painting.

I did animals and still lifes, but I kept coming back to drawing people. It's because I'm an introvert, I think. I'm naturally shy and that's why I'm always looking at people to see how they behave and what's going on with them. What is it that they are thinking but not saying? What are their lives like, their experiences? Who are they? Every time I look at someone, I'm drawing them mentally. That's how I process people. It's how I look at the world.

I'm always seeing people I'd like to draw, but I don't sketch in public because I don't like the attention it attracts. 'Artist in the park drawing' – it's a bit of a cliché. I know people mean well when they gather round to have a look, but it makes me feel uncomfortable.

Sometimes I'm too shy to ask people if I can draw them. It happened on the bus one time. I saw this girl and thought, 'I really want to draw her!'

But I didn't know how to go about approaching her. 'Can I draw you?' can sometimes be a hard thing to ask a stranger, and I didn't want her to think I was some sleazy douche bag artist guy. So I missed out.

I got around the disappointment by telling myself that I'd already mentally drawn her.

Creating an image

Every portrait I draw starts in my head. That's the difficult part, deciding on colour, composition, medium, paper and time… everything.

The easy part is putting it on paper, because it's already drawn in my head. I know which materials I need and where to get them, and I know how long the face is going to take me to draw. That's something I decide before I start and I stick to it. I wasn't taught to do it – it's just part of the process.

I get a feeling about the medium I want to use. It's a knowing vibe. In this book, I've used graphite, pastel, charcoal and ink. I go through phases. Pastels are my main thing right now, but I've been through a watercolour phase, a pencil phase and an ink phase in the past.

The drawing process

I see the face on the paper before I draw, then I'm just following what I already see, it's about trusting your instincts. You can't think, because if you think you make mistakes. If you just do, yes, you'll still make mistakes, but you can at least see them to correct them.

It definitely doesn't work if you overthink it. I made that mistake once, when I was drawing a portrait of the footballer Nigel Reo-Coker. I drew the outline, looked at it, thought, 'No,' rubbed it out and started again. I did that eighty times. It was wrong and it kept being wrong. I'd done portraits of him before and that was the problem: because I kept thinking, 'I want it to be as good as the others. I want it to surpass the others; it's got to be really good.'

Even after all that, I still wasn't that pleased with the result. That's why I trust my instincts.

right and following pages: *Nigel Reo-Coker.* Nigel is a guy who breaks the footballer stereotype: he has a genuine love of art and commissioned me to do pieces for some of his homes. I re-drew one portrait of him eighty times.

I always put the eyes in last. It sounds strange, I know, but I don't want them looking at me and I don't want to look at them for too long. Even if they're happy eyes or beautiful eyes, I put them in last. It's definitely true that the eyes are the windows to the soul.

People tell me all kinds of things when I'm drawing them. They worry that they're going to distract me, but when I say it's fine to talk, they really open up. That's great for me. I want to talk to them and profile them and get to know them as much as possible. However, I've been drawn and I didn't like it much, so I'm very sensitive to people's feelings when I'm drawing them. It can be intrusive to have someone examining you so closely.

My own worst critic

I scrutinize my work so much. Everything that leaves the studio, I've scrutinized more deeply than anyone else ever could. People often ask me, 'When is something finished?' Once I've sprayed it with a fixative, that's it. I don't go back to it after that. Even if you say it's good, I know what's wrong with it, but I just have to detach myself when it's done. It's never perfect, because perfect is never finished.

I'm developing and I'm imperfect, so I don't mind if there are imperfections in my work. Although I make sure to keep those imperfections to a minimum, I want people to see that a hand has drawn my art. I don't want it to look like it was made by a human photocopying machine.

Still, people have said of my work, 'This is clearly a photo that has just been through photoshop. I can see the photoshop markings.'

Well, no, it's not, and you can't. It's kind of flattering and insulting at the same time – but mostly funny.

Artistic influences

The painters I love most are the old master painters like Velázquez and Rembrandt, Michelangelo, Caravaggio and Rubens. When I want inspiration, I always go back to their work. That's the school I come from. They come the closest to painting the soul – they're that good. Right now I'm into John Singer Sargent. I love Sargent's work. He's the type of artist I dream of being.

When I was at sixth-form college, I got into the Czech Art Nouveau artist Alphonse Mucha. His work is incredible. He influenced me greatly. A lot of the Mucha-style work I did was in ink. I couldn't get enough of it.

Even now, every time I see a book on Mucha, I need to own it. I want to know everything about him.

One modern artist I am inspired by is Chuck Close. Close up, his photorealist portraits just look like a collection of scratches or circles, but when you stand back something wonderful happens and there's a realistic person looking at you. They're incredible.

how the artist works

preceding pages: *Freddie*. This portrait is of one of Ed's friends. I remember finding him quite mysterious at the time – I guess I expected him to be the total opposite to how he was. A really cool guy, who was so patient throughout the sitting.
left: *Neville*. Neville is a friend of mine from university, I've drawn him a few times.

Phillip

Life as an Artist

When people ask for my advice about becoming an artist, I always say, 'Is it something you really want to do?' Because it's not straightforward. It's not a career that happens overnight; you need time. Time to develop and understand who you are artistically. I always say, 'Draw every day. It will help you figure things out and find your style.'

After sixth-form college, I went to Central Saint Martins to do an art foundation course. Then I took a year out to go travelling, and then I went back to Saint Martins to do a degree in art and design. I kind of liked it there, but I don't think I'm really cut out for formal education. Maybe I could teach, though. I recently did a talk at a school and led a drawing workshop – and I enjoyed it a lot. I thought, 'This is so much fun, I could do this!'

When I first left Saint Martins, I worked all over London doing all kinds of jobs. As time went on and I started getting more commissions for my art, I was able to work fewer and fewer hours and focus on my drawing instead. Finally, I just worked weekends.

I've never been good at marketing my work. I think it's a general issue for artists: you want people to see your work but without exploiting yourself. It can be a balancing act. I've always just got on with the drawing and hoped – perhaps naively – that that would be enough. It doesn't come naturally to me to say, 'My name's Phil and this is what I do!'

A few years ago, Ed's dad John noticed this and gave me a telling-off and told me to get serious. He gave me a letter and said, 'Read this on the train.'

Once I was on the train, I took a deep breath and read it. In the letter he basically said, 'If you want to do this, do it. If you don't, don't.'

I actually see Ed's parents as my surrogate parents; they are the best mentors.

'Ah well,' I thought, 'at least he cares. He wrote it because he cares.' John and Imogen have always had really good advice and direction for me.

As painful as it was, I followed his advice and managed to get myself out there a bit more. I'm still working on that – and it all still feels new to me – but it's happening, especially now I've got people to help me with it. The work is coming through more regularly and I can pick and choose a bit more.

I think I'm getting there.

It's a really good feeling.

preceding pages: *Nadine*. She has the most beautiful, infectious smile.
following pages: *Neville*. Neville used to work in the Science Museum as a kids' entertainer, where he did live demos in the toyshop section, blowing up this plastic gooey type of slime. It sets hard when you blow it up. He blew up this bubble, then put his head inside it – don't try this at home! It's a really old portrait, I did it about seven years ago, but I've always liked it.

Phillip Butah timeline

1998
Youngest prizewinner of Young Artists' Britain:
The Prince of Wales's Young Artists' Award

2005
Exhibited at Windows Gallery, London

2006
Graduated with a BA in Fine Art from Central Saint
Martins College of Art and Design

2008
Named an up-and-coming figure in The Powerlist:
Britain's 100 most influential black people

2009
Commissioned to paint a portrait of HRH The Prince
of Wales
Member of the judging panel for Young Brits at Art

2011
Produced artwork for + album by Ed Sheeran

2014
Produced artwork for x album by Ed Sheeran

following pages: *Linford Christie*. I was fortunate enough to be given a ticket to a premiere of a film. My sister had a ticket but she didn't want to go. Linford Christie was sitting right behind me in the cinema. I just thought, 'This is my chance. I've got to ask him if I can draw him.' He's a childhood hero. So I asked him. 'Yeah,' he said, 'Send me an email. Speak to my assistant.' So I did. He got back to me and invited me down to a training session. We started talking and he told me all kinds of things. I couldn't believe it. 'This is not happening,' I thought. 'Wow!' He is such a cool guy.

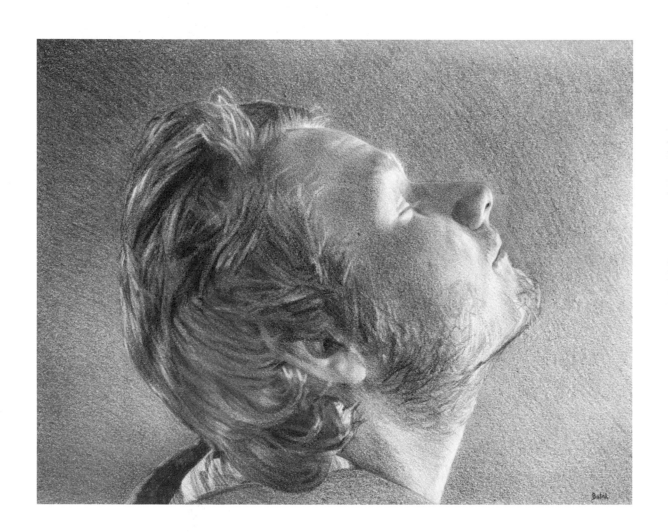

list of the artist's works

PAGE 1
Ink pen on paper.
This was for the
Afire Love cover.

PAGE 17
Coloured pastel
on coloured paper.
Ed is two years
old; he has such
innocence.

PAGE 22
Coloured pastel on coloured paper.
Ed's in a recording booth very early
on here.

PAGE 28
Graphite on paper.
John Sheeran, Ed's
dad, just relaxing
at home.

PAGE 30
Coloured wax pastel on coloured paper.
This is at Ed's house, Ed had just done
a radio interview on *No Hats, No Trainers*
and we were listening to hip hop together.

PAGE 34
Charcoal on paper. Ed's in the recording
studio recording his first songs.

PAGE 40
Ink, watercolour
pens and pencil on
paper. I wanted to
try something a bit
different. It's mixed
media and quite
a departure from
my other works.

PAGE 49
Graphite on paper.
I drew this when
Ed was recording
in Jake Gosling's
Sticky Studios. It
was just a doodle
to pass the time.

PAGE 50
Graphite on paper. This is a preliminary sketch. In the final piece I wanted to show how Ed was growing more confident.

PAGE 53
Carbon paper. We were just hanging out at my house, just vibing, Ed on guitar and me drawing.

PAGE 58
Coloured pastels on coloured paper. Ed's in the studio, working on collaborations.

PAGE 62
Watercolour pen on paper. We were just chilling out and jamming at mine.

PAGE 66
Graphite on paper. I started this at Jake's recording studio, but finished it at home.

PAGE 70
Graphite on paper. This was on the video set for 'You need me, I don't need you'. It was eventually used for the single's artwork.

PAGE 74
Graphite on paper. This was for 'The A-Team' single but wasn't used in the end. The two and three on the fingers represent Ed's collaborations.

PAGE 79
Coloured pastel on paper. I met Jamal Edwards through Ed, and he agreed to sit for this portrait.

PAGE 84
Graphite stick on paper. At Ed's house in Suffolk. The working drawings are on pages 190–93. I visualize the shape of the head on the paper before I start working, then I always create the eyes last.

PAGE 88
Biro on paper. The *No. 5 Collaborations Project* artwork, drawn in Jake Gosling's studio. Ed was nervous about being on the cover so I created the work as him slowly revealing himself.

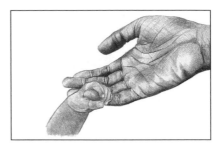

PAGE 94
Graphite on paper. This was one of the options for the 'Small Bump' artwork. I didn't want it to be too corny. The record company chose a different version to this in the end. I prefer this one though.

PAGE 102
Black pastel on coloured paper. Part of a series for *+*, it shows Ed emerging from the gigging circuit and into the public eye. I wanted it to become iconic.

PAGE 107
Watercolour brush and pencil on paper. Ed had built a Lego house in his studio and I thought it would be cool to show him as a Lego man.

PAGE 123
Wax pencils on paper. Ed headlining Shepherd's Bush Empire in October 2011 – a long-held ambition of his.

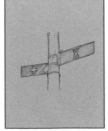

PAGE 126
Graphite on paper. One of the artworks for *x*, it's about being in New York, feeling slightly lost.

PAGE 132
Graphite on paper. Ed playing in Madison Square Garden. He looked so small; it's such a massive, phenomenal venue.

PAGE 135
Graphite on paper.
This was originally
just my own drawing
to support the 'Sing'
single, but Ed loved
it and decided to
use it too.

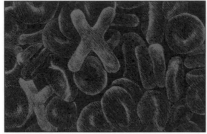

PAGE 140
Watercolour pen on paper. I wanted to
show the structure of blood really close
up. This actually extends way beyond the
page but I like how it's cropped to focus
on the 'x' and make it seem more medical.

PAGE 148
Mixed media. In
Ed's garden, just
chilling in the sun.

PAGE 153
Biro on paper. This
was an idea for
*No. 5 Collaborations
Project*, I didn't like
how I'd created the
eye though.

PAGE 156
Pen on paper. The award shows
a representation of being famous
and everything (good and bad)
that comes along with it.

PAGE 159
Coloured pastels
on coloured paper.
I wanted to get across
how transformative
Ed's fame and success
has been, it's just
changed his world.

PAGE 163
Coloured pastel
on coloured paper.
This is one of a
series. It's fairly
fragmented but
finished and I like
the feeling that
it captures.

PAGE 168
Coloured pastel on coloured paper.
I've made several portraits of Ashley
(Walters, also known as Asher D),
he has such a great face to draw.

PAGE 173
Coloured pastel
on coloured paper.
I've drawn other
portraits of Nigel
Reo-Coker too. He
really appreciates
the artistic process.

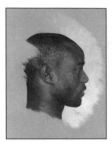

PAGE 175
Black and white
pastel on coloured
paper. Pastel enabled
me to capture hyper-
real textures. I'm
ready for the next
challenge now.

PAGE 176
Coloured pastel on coloured paper.
This was drawn from life and Freddie
(Ed's friend) was so relaxed during
the sitting.

PAGE 178
Black and white
pastel on coloured
paper. Drawing my
friends allows me
to experiment with
compositions and
colour schemes.

PAGE 180
Black and white pastel on coloured
paper. I like how this captures the split
second, immediate moment when my
friend Nadine smiles.

PAGE 184
Coloured pastel on coloured paper. I was
fascinated by the idea of Neville's head
contained so perfectly within the bubble,
with colours swimming around it.

PAGE 188
Coloured pastel on coloured paper.
I sketched the basis for this when Linford
(Christie) was training top athletes at Brunel
University. It was good to see someone
like him passing on his knowledge and
expertise to young athletes.

acknowledgements

From Ed & Phillip:

Special thanks to Stuart Camp, Will Ashurst, Andy Wells, and all at Rocket Music.

Thank you to the Octopus Publishing team. Hannah Knowles for having the vision to make this a reality. Rebecca Cripps, Emma Smith at Smith & Gilmour, Christie Goodwin, Pauline Bache, Giulia Hetherington, Caroline Brown, Karen Baker, Karla Pett, Frances Johnson and Peter Hunt.

Separately, Ed would like to thank:

I'd like to thank all my family, friends and fans for supporting me and making my music a success.

Separately, Phillip would like to thank:

I would like to express my gratitude to God for my life, family and friends and all His blessings. I'm incredibly humbled to have been given the opportunity to make this book.

Thanks to Nick Smith, Leon Thompson, Darren and Lisa Coleman, Tarkan Paphiti and Offset Media team, Tammy McKendrick, Paul Blake, Dewi and Natasha Bruce-Konuah.

Love to Jamal Edwards, for supporting this project from the beginning. Isaac Densu, thanks for all your support and hard work, love bro.

To my mum, no one has done more than you to make my dreams come true. You are always there for me. You provided everything in order to make it possible for me to pursue my art from school days till now. Always putting us first no matter what. I love you so much. Love and thanks to my sister Ruthie, you've always supported me, with kind words, comfort and love.

Huge love to John and Imogen Sheeran for your guidance, love and support and always making time for me.

Thanks to my friends for all your support, advice and love.

Lastly thank you to Ed, it's such an honour for me to have made this book with you. You continue to inspire me, not just the way you conceive the songs and sing them but you're always so gracious and humble with your success. Your talent has given my work a worldwide audience. Thank you for always supporting me throughout, lots of love bro.

index

index

index

index

publisher's acknowledgements

The publisher would like to thank Stuart Camp, Andy Wells, Emma Smith, Rebecca Cripps, Kate Moore, Christie Goodwin, Patrick Cusse and John and Imogen Sheeran for their involvement in making this book.

In most cases, artworks and photographs have been supplied by Phillip Butah, Ed, John and Imogen Sheeran. Additional credits are as follows:
10 above left Rubber Soul by The Beatles, 1965, Parlophone © Calderstone Productions Ltd, photography by Robert Freeman; 10 above right The Marshall Mathers LP by Eminem, 2000, © Aftermath Entertainment & Interscope Records/Polydor Records & Universal Music Group, art direction Jason Noto, photography by Jonathan Mannion; 10 below left Moondance by Van Morrison, 1970, Warner Brothers © Warner Music UK Ltd, photography by Elliot Landy; 10 below right Madman Across the Water by Elton John, 1971, DJM Records © Mercury Records Ltd; 12 Phil Mead; 25 Kevin Mazur/WireImage Getty Images; 33 Barbara Lindberg; 42-3 Tabatha Fireman/Redferns/Getty Images; 57 Christie Goodwin; 65 Yui Mok/PA Wire/Press Association Images; 73 courtesy Crisis.org.uk, photo Tony Hall; 81 courtesy Flypoet Entertainment; 83 courtesy War Child, photo Andy Willsher; 91 Sylvie Varnier; 101 Christie Goodwin; 108 Christie Goodwin; 111 courtesy Sticky Company; 113 Christie Goodwin; 114 David M Benett/Getty Images for Fudge Urban; 119 Christie Goodwin; 120 edsheeran.com; 124 photo courtesy of BASCA © Mark Allan; 129 Dave Thompson/WPA Pool/Getty Images; 130 Christie Goodwin; 136–7 Christie Goodwin; 139 Kevork Djanasezian/Getty Images; 144 Christie Goodwin; 160 Christie Goodwin.